D1794916

The Happy art of Catching Men

You are holding a reproduction of an original work that is in the public domain in the United States of America, and possibly other countries. You may freely copy and distribute this work as no entity (individual or corporate) has a copyright on the body of the work. This book may contain prior copyright references, and library stamps (as most of these works were scanned from library copies). These have been scanned and retained as part of the historical artifact.

This book may have occasional imperfections such as missing or blurred pages, poor pictures, errant marks, etc. that were either part of the original artifact, or were introduced by the scanning process. We believe this work is culturally important, and despite the imperfections, have elected to bring it back into print as part of our continuing commitment to the preservation of printed works worldwide. We appreciate your understanding of the imperfections in the preservation process, and hope you enjoy this valuable book.

THE HAPPY ART OF CATCHING MEN

THE HAPPY ART
OF
CATCHING MEN

A STORY OF GOOD SAMARITANSHIP

BY
REV. R. J. PATTERSON, A.B., LL.B.
Trinity College, Dublin
Founder of the Catch-My-Pal Movement

"From henceforth thou shalt catch men"

HODDER & STOUGHTON
NEW YORK
GEORGE H. DORAN COMPANY

HV 5448
.P3

Copyright, 1914, by
GEORGE H. DORAN COMPANY

DEDICATED
TO THE MEMORY OF MY AUNT,
MRS. HELENA PATTERSON,
THE MANSE, BRAY, CO. WICKLOW, IRELAND,
WHO WAS A LOVING MOTHER TO ME,
AND WHO, BY GOING ABOUT DOING GOOD,
TAUGHT ME, WHEN A BOY,
THE SECRET OF GOOD SAMARITANSHIP;

ALSO TO
MY DEAR WIFE,
WHO URGED ME TO RESIGN
MY MINISTRY IN ARMAGH
THAT I MIGHT GO OUT ON
THIS CRUSADE,
AND WHO, IN LOVING LONELINESS,
IS DOING HER PART
WHILE I WANDER ABOUT THE WORLD

PREFACE

THE story told in this little book is considered one of the most remarkable in the records of social reform. I have told this story hundreds of times all over Ireland, and in many parts of Great Britain and Holland and America. In the summer of 1913 I travelled twenty-one thousand miles in the United States and Canada that I might bring its message of hope to the fallen and to those who are lifting the fallen. The work of the Catch-my-Pal movement is recorded not only in this book, but in countless redeemed lives in places so far apart as Inverness and Sydney, Stratford-on-Avon and Toronto, Armagh and Kingston (Jamaica), Arnheim in Holland and Portland (Oregon).

That there is need for such work in America is testified by the fact that I have been asked to come to America again for a campaign in various districts, including two months in Chicago. Indeed, I have been surprised at the manner in which social reformers in the United States and Canada have taken to the movement.

As far as legislation is concerned America is much ahead of the United Kingdom. Local Option has at last begun to get a footing in Scotland, as the Scottish Temperance Act of 1913, which is a Local Option Act, will be put into operation in that country in 1920. It is hoped that such a revolution will take place there through the Act that the rest of the United Kingdom will rise and demand similar treatment at the hands of the Imperial Parliament.

But while the United States' Legislation is greatly

in advance of that in the United Kingdom is it going too far to say that it seems as if *too much stress is laid on legislation and too little stress on moral suasion?* I have been told by some of the foremost Temperance authorities that the time for pledge-signing in America is long past! In other words, the time for moral suasion is long past, and legislation will now complete the programme of the Temperance Reformers. When I was in America in 1913 I addressed many meetings in connection with Rescue Missions, in which I saw men as low down through drink as any I have ever seen in the United Kingdom. Is it not necessary to get them to sign the pledge? Surely moral suasion is necessary wherever men and women are down or going down? Every time I had an opportunity of going along the streets of American towns, at the close of my meetings, I went to the doors of the saloons to see things for myself. I saw that the saloons were usually well filled and, in many cases, crowded. Wherever there are saloons there is drinking. Wherever there is drinking there is drunkenness. Wherever there is drunkenness there is much need of saving the drunkards. And as long as there is need of saving the drunkards there is need of moral suasion. And as long as moral suasion is applied to the solution of the drink problem there will be need of pledge-signing.

But, where do the drunkards come from? From among the moderate drinkers. In most cases the moderate drinkers require more moral suasion than the drunkards. The drink bill of the United States shows that the moderate drinkers can be counted by millions. All these millions need moral suasion. *A great campaign of pledge-signing among these moderate drinkers is absolutely necessary if the United States are to be saved from the drink curse.*

One Sunday night I addressed an audience of about twelve hundred persons in a "dry" town. I asked every person, who DID NOT KNOW A DRINKER,

PREFACE

to hold up the right hand. One person, an old man,
held up his hand. I asked him, "Do you mean to say
you do not know a drunkard?" He said, "I don't know
one in this town." I then asked him, "How long have
you lived in this town?" And he answered, "I'm a
stranger here." Naturally I remarked to the meeting,
"When you were a 'wet' town you drank in the open.
Now you are 'dry' you drink on the sly." Evidently
there was much "shipping" of drink into that town.
Wherever there is shipping of drink into "dry" towns
or districts there is need of moral suasion and, conse-
quently, of pledge-signing campaigns, as well as in the
"wet" districts.

The slogan is now being sounded, *"A Saloonless
Nation in 1920!"* In seven years what thousands of
men, women and children can be slain by drink! Must
we wait on legislation? Can we not save thousands
before 1920? Will the hoped-for legislation of 1920,
if it is practically realised, save the drinkers and
drunkards of to-day? Surely NOW is the accepted
time for them? Surely NOW is the day of *their* salvation?

I have found that there are hundreds of drunkards
who are only waiting for someone to come along and
lift them up. Good Samaritanship is not out of date.
*As in the United Kingdom, so in the United States,
there are great numbers of drunkards who are ready
to stand on their feet again if they are only asked to
stand.* A campaign of Good Samaritanship among
the drinkers and drunkards of the land will turn all
those whom it saves from the enemy into volunteers
in the fight for a Saloonless Nation in 1920, and, at the
same time, it will, perhaps more than anything else,
help to form that irresistible PUBLIC OPINION
against which the gates of the Licensed National Curse
shall not be able to stand.

If the publication of this little book in America
tends in any way to bring about such a campaign, I

PREFACE

shall be grateful as one who is "seeing of the travail of his soul."

It is a matter of regret to me that I have had to use the first personal pronoun so often; but I think my seeming egotism will be forgiven when it is remembered that I am telling a story which gathered about myself in a way that is a great and growing surprise to me.

I thank God for giving me the story to tell, and I send it out in the earnest hope that it may help to leave the world at least a little better than it found it.

ROBERT J. PATTERSON.

PITTSBURGH, PA., March, 1914.

CONTENTS

xi

xii CONTENTS

THE HAPPY ART OF CATCHING MEN

The Happy Art of Catching Men

CHAPTER I

SNAKES

ONE day as I was walking along one of the lovely boulevards of Bay View, Michigan, in August, 1913, two ladies met me and stopped me. One of them asked me, "Can you tell me where The Wren's Nest is?" This is the name of one of the many dainty little lakeside homes in that quiet inland holiday resort. I said, "I have travelled three thousand miles from Ireland to New York, and another thousand miles from New York to Bay View, and do you think I have travelled all those four thousand miles to look for such diminutive things as wrens' nests in such a prodigious country as yours?"

The good lady looked at me and said, "Are you an Irishman?" and I said, "Yes." "And are you the Irishman who is going to address our Summer Assembly to-morrow?" I said, "Yes." She peered at me, her eyes betokening wonder. "So you are the Irishman who is to speak to-morrow?" And again I answered, "YES!" The two ladies then gazed at me in such a way as to make me feel that I was a curiosity. As I parted from them and, as they were still within earshot, I heard one of them say to the other, "I suppose he will be talking to us about SNAKES." All people know that St. Patrick drove the snakes out of Ireland, and some people, when they hear the name of Ireland, think immediately about St. Patrick and the snakes.

When I got up to speak at the Assembly I told what the ladies said the previous day, and proceeded,— "That lady who said she supposed I was going to talk about snakes was much nearer the truth than she thought she was. For I came from Armagh, the City of St. Patrick. Our Irish Patron Saint established the Christian Church in Armagh a thousand years before Columbus came from my side of the Atlantic to discover your country for you. It has always been said that 'Saint Pathrick was a gintleman, and came of dacent people.' And so we all like to claim kinship with him. Armagh is the ecclesiastical capital of my country. The Cardinal Archbishop of the Roman Catholic Church lives there, and the Primate of the Episcopal Church lives there. I was the senior of three young Presbyterian Ministers in the city, and I looked upon myself, though nobody else did, as the Archbishop of the Presbyterians. Now, the Roman Catholics say that St. Patrick was a Roman Catholic, and the Episcopalians say that he was an Episcopalian, and the Presbyterians say that he was a Presbyterian. And while the Roman Catholic Archbishop on the one side, and the Episcopal Archbishop on the other side, were fighting about the Chair of St. Patrick, I, as the senior Presbyterian Minister, quietly SAT in the Chair. I claim to be the successor of St. Patrick. It is said that St. Patrick drove the snakes out of Ireland. But there is one snake he did not drive out, the most deadly of all the snakes, the most poisonous of all snakes, *the most sneaky snake that ever wriggled its way through Irish grass or through American sagebrush*. I mean the DRINK TRAFFIC. I am out to club that snake. God has placed in my hand a club called Catch-my-Pal, and I claim to be at least one of St. Patrick's successors in this snake business."

I proceeded to tell the Assembly the story recorded in the following chapters. I hope my appeal resulted in some of my hearers giving up the drink, and in setting them and others about doing something to save their fellows who are in the coils of this snake. May the reading of this story be the means of setting many about the doing of SOMETHING to deliver this great land from her greatest curse, so that she may be indeed God's Own Country, and the Land of the Free.

CHAPTER II

"Roast Missionary"

WHEN I was a boy at school I had a great desire to be an African missionary. David Livingstone was my hero. My chums made fun of me and often told me how the cannibals would eat me. They called me "Roast Missionary." Perhaps no boy ever enjoyed his nickname more than I enjoyed mine.

I went into Trinity College, Dublin, with that desire still strong in me. I passed to the New College, Edinburgh; and there, in the first budding of the Students' Missionary Movement, I dedicated myself to missionary work, wherever God would call me.

Several things prevented my going to the foreign field when I left the Assembly's College, Belfast; and, three months after license, I found myself ordained as minister of one of the Presbyterian Churches in the city of Armagh, about twelve miles from where I was born.

While I was in Armagh my ministry was largely devoted to fighting the drink evil and to fostering the missionary idea. I gave so much attention to pleading the cause of missions that I was told by members of my congregation that I should go out as a missionary myself.

Many a time I felt I should do as was suggested, but the way did not become open. My wife's health was such as to need my almost constant attention. But I began to feel that *a call was coming to leave the stated ministry* of the congregation. I was North of Ireland Secretary of the Religious Tract Society, and

4

in this capacity I had occasion to go over many miles of road on a motor bicycle. Sometimes I rode from thirty to sixty miles in a day, and in such journeys I saw many tramps on life's highways and byways, men, women and children, for whose souls no one seemed to care. I longed to do something to seek and save them. The longing became so intense that I said to one of the elders of my congregation at the close of a morning service in June, 1909: "I think I'll not be your minister much longer." He said: "Why, what makes you think so?" I told him what I had seen along the roads, and how I felt that I was getting a call to be a missionary—*a missionary to the tramps of the country.*

A few weeks after that Sunday the Catch-my-Pal movement began. I believe it came in answer to my great desire. I did not go out as a missionary to the tramps on the road, but I went out as *a missionary to prevent men and women from becoming tramps.* Drink is the chief cause of trampdom, and I know that many of those who have been saved from drink by this movement have been saved from the highways and hedges.

The MISSIONARY CALL had come. I resigned my charge in Armagh. If I have not become a "roast" missionary on a cannibal island or in the heart of Africa, it is because there was another purpose for me. The Catch-my-Pal movement has snatched many a man, and many a woman and child, from the jaws of *the cannibal, Drink.*

CHAPTER III

A City's Awakening

For seventeen years I was minister of The Mall Presbyterian Church in Armagh city.

From the beginning of my ministry I was deeply interested in temperance work, and one of the regrets of my heart was that, while our temperance meetings were usually well attended, I never saw at one of them a drunk person, or a person accustomed to drink to excess. Our meetings were largely attended by those who were predisposed to temperance, and at the close of each meeting many an earnest soul must have felt that very little was done to save the fallen or to redeem the neighbourhood.

It often seemed to me that the "Trade" stood at its corners every day and every night and laughed at most of the attempts of the Church to dislodge it from its position; and it was no wonder I was interested in the question a brother minister asked me one night, at a meeting of the Clerical Club of the Presbytery of Armagh: *"How is it that after nineteen hundred years of Christian history the Devil seems to have more power in the world to-day than Christ has?"* That question bothered me very much. I could not get rid of it. The night on which I was asked it I could hardly sleep. It was the first question knocking at my heart on the following morning; and, as I walked down the street and saw so many saloons in the most ancient Christian city in the United Kingdom, I felt there was a vital connection between the drink question and the minister's question. *In my heart I vowed that*

6

if God would show me the way I would do at least one man's part to take the laugh out of the cheek of the trade. Three weeks after I made that vow the Catch-my-Pal Movement was born in that selfsame street.

About this time The Pioneer Movement, founded by Father Cullen, S.J., Dublin, which worked wonderful things in other parts of Ireland, was introduced to Armagh by Father Sheerin, C.C. He became the talk of the city as he gathered a great band of men and women around him on the total abstinence platform. So fast were the strides made by the Roman Catholics of the city in total abstinence reform that it was said the Protestants were almost at a standstill. This state of matters both gladdened and saddened me, and I became earnest in prayer that something might be done to arouse our Protestant population.

I went to see Father Sheerin in his house, and I asked him to come to see me in mine. We were constantly meeting on the street, and our talk always turned on the temperance problem. Several times I asked him to let me know the secret of his success in dealing with his people, but I never had any satisfaction from him in our wayside conversations. One day I saw him going into a shop. I followed him. We talked temperance again. I put my hand on his shoulder and, looking him in the face, I said:

"Father Sheerin, I'll not let you out of this shop till you tell me what is the secret of your success in dealing with your people on the temperance question."

He answered in his meek and quiet way: "Well, to tell you the truth, I have no secret except just this— *the people think I am in earnest about it.*"

That was all I got from Father Sheerin. But it was enough. I was in earnest too, but not earnest enough. I was more in earnest when I went out of that shop than when I went into it.

I did not get the Catch-my-Pal idea from the priest. I got it in that well-spring of inspiration, the Gospel

7

of St. John. *Our holy religion was started on Catch-my-Pal lines.* Our Lord caught Andrew, and Andrew caught Peter and brought him to Jesus. Then He caught Philip, and Philip caught Nathaniel and brought him to Jesus. "And He must needs go through Samaria." Why? Because there was a defiled woman coming to a well, and He wanted to catch and captivate her for purity of life.

> "Samaria's humble daughter,
> Who paused to hear, beside her well,
> Lessons of love and truth which fell
> Softly as Shiloh's flowing water;
> And saw, beneath His pilgrim's guise,
> The Promised One, so long foretold
> By holy seer and bard of old,
> Revealed before her wondering eyes." (Whittier)

When she was caught she went and caught her pals and brought them to Jesus, and there was a Revival in Sychar on Catch-my-Pal lines. I got Catch-my-Palism from Jesus.

But I got just a little extra enthusiasm from the priest, and it was that I needed. It is *that* the ministers of all the churches need, for if they were all enthusiastic about the solution of this, the biggest social and Christian problem of our day, I believe *the drink evil would be shaken to its foundations in a single year.*

CHAPTER IV

A Joke Turned to the Glory of God

I HAD no more idea how I might put my new enthusiasm into practice than I had how to start a transatlantic aeroplane service. But, if an earnest desire to DO SOMETHING means prayer, my heart was filled with an earnest prayer for guidance and wisdom. And an answer came to me in a way that was not to be mistaken, on *the 13th of July, 1909.* If I felt every day, as I went along the street, that the trade was bubbling over with laughter at me, on that day I found the way to prick at least some of the bubbles.

As everyone knows, the 12th of July is a great day among the members of the Orange Order. The Orangemen of Ireland are speedily being changed into a great Total Abstinence Society; but I fear it used to be characteristic of some of them, as of many other Orders, to imbibe somewhat freely on their annual holiday. On the 13th there was usually much penitence in many quarters, penitence begotten largely by soreness of head, and not seldom by soreness of heart. Many men who lived perfectly sober lives all the rest of the year considered they should have a little latitude on the 12th; and on the 13th they pulled themselves together again. As a minister I found I was asked to give and witness more pledges in the second half of July than at any other time of the year.

On the 13th of July, 1909, I was going home to my Manse in the main street of Armagh, when I saw six men standing at a lamp-post, around which it was the custom to talk and smoke. As I drew near, one of

9

them, John Elliott, detached himself from the others, passed me, and went down a side street. Just after passing he looked back at me, and, pointing with his left thumb over his shoulder at the lamp-post, he said, in a cheery, jaunty manner: "There are some men at the lamp-post, yir rivirince, an' you ought to get them to sign the pledge." Then John went on. His remark was seemingly a joke; but it was *a joke turned to the glory of God.* It was like a spark falling from a passing train in the dry grass of the prairie, and soon the whole prairie was on fire.

I called, "John! John! Come here!" He stopped and hesitatingly came back to me. I said:

"Come along, John, and let us see what we can do with these fellows." And we two approached the five.

"Men," I said. "here is one of yourselves, and he says he thinks it would be a good thing if I got you to sign the pledge. What do you say?"

One said one thing, and another said another thing; and after about ten minutes' talk about the evils of drink and the blessings of sobriety, I got the six to agree that it would be a good thing to sign.

"All right, men," I said, "you'll all come over to my house there with the white door and sign the pledge——"

"Oh, no! your reverence, we will not do it so quick as that," said one.

"But," I answered. "I was not going to ask you to do it now. I don't want you to do it in a hurry. If you do, you will likely undo it in a hurry. If you had not interrupted I was going to say that I want you all to come together to my house on next Friday evening, at nine o'clock, when the curfew rings in the Cathedral tower up there. Go home and think about it; talk about it; pray about it; and come with your minds made up on Friday at nine o'clock."

"Well, we'll go one by one, your reverence. We'll not all go together."

10

"If you don't all come together I will not have you at all," I answered.

Why did I say so? As my Manse was in the centre of the city, I was the most convenient minister for pledge-signing purposes. I found that all kinds of people came to sign the pledge with me, especially people belonging to other ministers. I believe many persons would rather sign the pledge with any other minister than their own, as it is not the part of the other minister to look after them to see whether they keep the pledge or not. I found also that many of those who took the pledge from me did so, not because they wanted to give up the drink, but because they had lost their jobs through taking too much, and they thought the best way to reinstate themselves was to get pledges from a minister to show to their employers. When they went back to their work they went back to their "nibbling and tasting" till they were warned again, and came back for another pledge. After several years' experience of such pledge-giving I believed that, on the average, about seven out of every ten persons who signed in private soon broke their pledges, and that *private pledge-signing was almost useless as a means of social reform.*

I saw an opportunity at the lamp-post, and I thank God for giving me the eyes to see it and the hand to grasp it. What was my opportunity? Six men were there, and I said to myself, "Here are six men, and if I can get them all *to sign in one another's presence,* each one will immediately find himself supported by a public opinion formed by five of his companions; and if one of them begins to go down he will find the arms of a brotherhood of five to buoy him up in the day of his temptation; *by himself he will fall, but in a brotherhood he will stand.*" Then I felt determined, and said in my heart: "In the name of God I'll not let these men go!"

We reasoned and we wriggled over the pledge-taking for some minutes, and at last I made my final appeal. "Men, do have some commonsense. If a servant maid in that house over there were going to light a fire with six dry sticks, and if she held one stick over a gas jet till it was alight and then put it into the grate *by itself*, what would happen?"

"It would go out," said the men.

"Yes, and if she did the same with the second stick, what would happen?"

"It would go out."

"Yes. And so it would be with each of the six sticks. But if she arranged some dry paper properly in the middle of the grate, and put the six sticks properly on the paper, and the coal on the sticks, and then put a match to the paper, she would soon have a delightful fire. And I want you all to come to my house on Friday next at curfew; and, as you are 'dry' to-night and will be 'drier' on Friday, *I'll arrange the six of you together*, and put a total abstinence match to you, and then we'll have a lovely total abstinence fire that will warm the heart of our old city."

Those six men were not drunkards. John Elliott, James Allen, James Farr, Robert Graham, Cecil Matson, and William Reid, were honourable, respectable, industrious men, who were not total abstainers. The 12th was past, and they were open to an appeal. The appeal came to them and they responded to it. They promised they would come, all together, for the lighting of the total abstinence fire.

I bade them good-night, and went home with my mind and heart all astir with a problem. It was Tuesday. The men promised to come on Friday. Would they keep their promise? That was *their* problem. What should I do with them if they came? That was *my* problem.

I had arranged to be out of Armagh on the Thursday and Friday to do work for the Religious Tract Society. The friends of that Society in Coleraine were expecting me. I did not go. I couldn't. Why? Because the problem of the six men had me in its grip. *It was a time for prayer, and I prayed, as perhaps I never prayed before,* that the men might come, and for wisdom that I might deal wisely with them when they came.

CHAPTER V

KINDLING A FIRE AT CURFEW

I DID not see one of the men between Tuesday and Friday; and on Friday I could do nothing but think of them. Would they come? What should I do with them?

When the curfew bell began to ring at nine o'clock my heart began to thump with a great expectancy. Would the men come? I waited almost ten minutes. Would they come? There was a knock! Who was it? I ran and opened the door, and, there, on the doorstep, were the six men! My heart rejoiced that *the six brave men had kept their word*. I threw the door wide open, welcomed each with a warm handshake, showed them into the dining-room, and there, around the table, we seven sat down, looked at each other in some surprise, and began our *first Catch-my-Pal Conference!*

We settled down into serious talk, and I made this statement to the men: "While it is the moderate drinker who is the real curse of the country as far as the drink problem is concerned—for, if there were no moderate drinkers there could be no immoderate ones—at the same time, it is the immoderate drinkers who make the drink problem the great, outstanding social problem of our day. *LET THOSE WHO MAKE THE PROBLEM SOLVE IT.* Let the drinkers take the pledge and go and get their pals to do the same. Let the responsibility of saving drinkers be left largely on the shoulders of the drinkers themselves. Let the drinkers be inspired with the idea that *even they* are their brothers' keepers, and that *even they* are expected by God to leave the world not worse but better than they found it."

I explained as well as I could how men could not live on negatives, and how something positive must be put before each man who wants to give up the drink. I said that abstinence was merely negative, that it was necessary that each one should DO something along a positive line, and that the best thing each one of them could do to enable him to keep his own pledge was to try to get others to take the pledge too. I told them what misery and squalor and disgrace drink was causing in our city, and that they could do much to mend matters. They were surprised when I told them that *they could do far more to solve the drink problem in the city than any six ministers.* I told them how we found in the South African War, when it was almost too late, that the frontal attack was fatal to the success of our British arms, and how we resorted to the flank movement, by which we won Pretoria. I told them how most men who drank were prepared for the frontal attack made on them by ministers; how they avoided ministers; and how all the bristles · of their natures stood on end to ward off a minister's approach. I told them how they could resort to the flank movement among their drinking pals; how they could talk with them, reason with them, and appeal to them, in a way that no minister could do. "Oh, men!" I said, "What happiness will come to your own firesides if you make up your minds you'll not let the drink there again! And what happiness you can bring to the firesides of others if each one of you will go out and bring other drinkers in!"

When I saw that these ideas were getting a hold of the men I ventured to say:

"Men, I'll not let one of you take the pledge to-night unless each one of you undertakes to go out and catch

15

another fellow, and come back here with him on to-morrow night week at nine o'clock."

The men looked at one another wondering if they should consent. I appealed to them: "Men go and do as I ask you. There are six of you to-night; and there will be twelve the next night; and there will be twenty-four the next; forty-eight the next; and ninety-six the next; and in a few weeks we shall have the whole country-side." I am now surprised at the audacity which led me to make this prophecy which was more than fulfilled.

The simplicity of this programme had an electrical effect upon the men. A new inspiration filled their bosoms; a new vision of life and duty their eyes; the "expulsive power of a new affection" began its work in their hearts. They itched to be out and at the other fellows!

The six then signed a pledge of total abstinence, and each solemnly promised to do his best to get another and bring him in. *I asked them to go for the biggest drinkers they could lay their hands on, as these were the men who needed salvation first and most, and whom Jesus would first seek out and save.* We knelt down round the table, and, in solemn prayer, commended ourselves and the work to the blessing of God as revealed in Jesus Christ.

In Norman times the curfew rang that the fires might be put out. That night in Armagh city the curfew rang from the Norman tower in St. Patrick's Cathedral that a fire might be kindled that, by the blessing of God, will never go out. Surely the Holy Spirit descended as in tongues of fire in that room! I feel a different man since I rose from my knees that night. My outlook on life is quite changed. I can say, "The Spirit of the Lord is upon me, because He hath anointed me to preach Good News to the drunkards, and the opening of the prison to them that are bound in drink." Out of that room there went *seven men on fire.* Six went into the street to do their wonderful work. I went into my study and said to my wife, "Do you know, something wonderful is going to happen." And, by the grace of God, the wonderful thing did happen, as hundreds of transformed firesides all over the world, but especially in my dear old Ireland, can testify to-day.

CHAPTER VI

In Double Harness

I HAD an anxious and weary week of waiting and of curiosity. On Saturday, 24th July, my heart thumped even more vigorously at curfew than it did on the 16th. But the week's wait was worth while. I was not disappointed. I had trusted the men, and I had my reward. A few minutes after nine o'clock I heard the expected knock. Again I ran to the door. There, on the step, were eleven men. One of the first six could not come, owing to his mother's illness; but, if Robert Graham did not catch his pal and *bring* him, he caught his pal and *sent* him. He was with us in spirit; so I had *twelve men*. My first Apostles carried out my instructions almost to the letter, for *they brought in some of the greatest drinkers in the city*. These men signed the total abstinence pledge, and each one undertook to bring in another. When they had signed we had our second conference.

I suggested that we should form ourselves into a society. One man said: "Let us wait for two or three weeks till we get in more men, and then we'll form ourselves into a society." But when I said that our Lord did not wait till He had a crowd of men around Him before He formed a society, but formed one with twelve men, whom He sent out to turn the world upside down, and that we could go out as Apostles of Total Abstinence and turn our city upside down as far as public opinion and practice in relation to the drink evil were concerned, nothing could keep

18

the men from being formed into a society. So we decided by resolution to form one there and then.

If you want to get a number of men to do something out of the ordinary line, tell them what great men they are, what great things they can do, and what great things you expect them to do; and, if they do not carry out your whole programme, they will do far more than ever they would have done if you had not "blown a head" on them.

Then we had to choose a name for our society. I suggested "Protestant Total Abstinence Union," and urged this name for the following reasons. I told the men I was not so narrow as to glory in sectarian differences, but that where a judicious use could be made of such differences, in a good cause, we ought to make such use of them. So I said we could not but admire how our Roman Catholic fellow-citizens were· making such strides on the highway of total abstinence, and that it was for us to get on the same highway, overtake them, and, if possible, outstrip them. The spirit of competition entered the blood of the men as they entered the ranks of the new society.

I said: "There will be no mention of Episcopacy, or of Methodism, or of Presbyterianism, or of any other 'ism,' in our society. Episcopacy as such will never save the world; Methodism as such will never save the world; Presbyterianism as such will never save the world; no 'ism' as such will ever save the world. But *the Spirit of Jesus in each 'ism'—THAT will save the world,* and we will all take our stand on a common platform of a united Protestantism for the sake of social reform. The churches have been going for one another's throats far too long, with regard to petty details that will be as chaff before the wind on the judgment day. Let us cease going for one another, and unite in going for the throat of the common enemy, the drink evil."

We decided to call our society "The Armagh Protestant Total Abstinence Union." After some weeks the movement extended beyond our city boundaries, and we changed the name to "The County Armagh Protestant Total Abstinence Union." Then, when it went outside the boundaries of the county, we enlarged the name by clipping part of it off, and called it "The Protestant Total Abstinence Union," a name we could go with anywhere.

Some of our critics think the society should have been placed on a basis broad enough to include our Roman Catholic fellow countrymen. All true social reform work is religious; and as temperance reform aims at the salvation of men's bodies, and our bodies are the temples of the Holy Ghost, true temperance reform work must be religious. The temple can be cleansed by Him only Whose temple it is. I wanted this movement to be a distinctly religious one from the first, and I hope it will continue to be so. In fact I consider it must continue to be so if it is to continue to exist. The Roman Catholics have their own Temperance Societies, such as The Pioneer Movement, The League of the Cross, the League of St. Patrick, The Father Mathew Society, etc., and I understand they are run on religious lines. Roman Catholics have their way of approaching God, and we Protestants have our way of approaching God, in devotional and other religious exercises. And, as Protestants and Roman Catholics cannot unite on the same devotional platform for prayer and praise and reading of Scripture and Gospel Temperance Addresses, *I thought it would be better to have a platform so narrow as to embrace all Protestants in religious union than to have one so broad as to embrace the Roman Catholics and have no religious union at all.*

There is no rivalry between the Roman Catholic Temperance Societies and The Protestant Total Abstinence Union except that of desire to save our land from drink. Indeed, I might say that if we are not

working in one organisation, and driving in single
harness, we are driving along our Irish city streets
and Irish highways in double harness, and I think we
make a rather attractive pair. In Lurgan the Master
of every Orange Lodge became a member of the
Union. At a great meeting of the Lurgan branch
a resolution was passed congratulating the local parish
priest upon his good work on behalf of total abstinence; and, in reply, the priest wrote a letter of thanks
and wished the Catch-my-Pal Union God-speed in its
endeavour to put down intemperance. Many Roman
Catholics, priests and laymen, have expressed their
satisfaction with our work, and we wish them every
blessing in all attempts to drive from our beloved land
the blackest curse that has ever blighted her fair face.

Having formed our Society and chosen our name,
we determined to go on with the work. I told the
men on that Saturday night that men were being lost
and that no time should be lost in saving them; that
I wanted them to go out and catch their pals and bring
them in to me on the following Monday night at half-
past nine o'clock. *The second batch of six caught fire!*
Twelve apostles of total abstinence knelt down round
the table to pray, and rose up to spread the fire.

CHAPTER VII

ECCLESIASTICAL STARCH

"PROTESTANT Total Abstinence Union" is our respectable, official name. It is our "Sunday-go-to-meeting" name. People usually feel somewhat confined in their Sunday clothes. To do hard, honest work, on Monday, we must get out of our Sunday garb and roll up our sleeves; and, as this movement soon proved itself very aggressive, I found it necessary to clothe it in some name suggestive of such a spirit.

On high days, and in official circles, we still are garbed in the name "Protestant Total Abstinence Union," but, in this "touch-the-button" age, life is too quick and too short to have time wasted in using high-sounding titles. So I sat down one day to weave a little short jacket for the movement with the keys of my typewriter. And when I had it woven I saw in the warp and woof of it the name *CATCH-MY-PAL*.

Where did I get the name? Christianity is a fisherman's movement. Our Lord said to Peter: "From henceforth thou shalt *catch* men." I took the word "catch" from the lips of Jesus. This is a fisherman's movement within the Churches. For successful fishing we must put on our hook the bait which will attract the fish we want to catch; and, as the word "pal" is used largely among men who drink with one another, especially in great centres of population, I thought it was the word for me. So I called the movement by the name Catch-my-Pal.

I thank the God of all wisdom for giving me this

name for the work. It arouses people's curiosity. It makes them talk, for it catches their tongues. It can be applied in innumerable ways to all departments of life. It looks quaint on a placard. Two ladies were passing down the street of an English town in a tram car. There was a large poster on a wall, announcing one of my meetings. One lady said to the other: "Do you know anything about this thing called Catch-my-Pal? Do you know if it is a new play? Is it a Drama?"

I do not believe the movement would have spread so widely in so short a time had it not been for this simple name.

Many objections have been raised to the name.

A minister in Scotland, when preaching a temperance sermon in 1910, referred to "a great temperance movement going on over in Ireland just now, whose name I refu-u-u-u-se to mention in this pulpit!"

A certain Irish bishop declared "the name was vulgar, and savoured of the gutter and the corner-boy."

A lady in a luxuriously-furnished drawing-room was asked by a minister much interested in the movement: "Have you joined the Catch-my-Pals yet?" She stiffened herself up in the most approved duchess manner, folded her arms, and exclaimed: "Oh, no!"

"And why have you not joined the movement yet?" inquired the minister.

"Ugh! On account of the name, you know. *It's so vulgar!*"

I fear that *much of our Church and social reform work is half damned with too much dignity.* Too much of it is steeped in the hue of patronage. We can never patronise a man into the kingdom of God. Thank God! there is still enough manliness and womanliness in the bosoms of the worst of us to detect the spirit of patronage whenever and wherever it would lift up its vulgar head over us, and to resent it and resist it. But, if we cannot patronise a soul into the kingdom, there are many souls on the verge of the kingdom and we must beware lest we patronise them away from it. The sooner we get the ecclesiastical starch out of our collars, the better for ourselves and for the kingdom of God. It is not ministers of whom I write, for *I have seen more ecclesiastical starch in the pews than ever I saw in the pulpit.* The time is coming quickly when this starch will not be tolerated within the Church.

But it is to be hoped that nothing vulgar will ever be tolerated within the Church of Christ. Some things may seem vulgar in our eyes which, in the eyes of God, are things of beauty. And "what God hath cleansed that call not thou common." God can lift the poor out of the dunghill and set him among princes. And what He can do with men He can do with words. The word "pal" is looked upon by fastidious people as slang; but what would they say if they met it among the prince-words of the dictionary? It is going up among those words to-day.

A learned Roman Catholic priest whom I met at a general temperance meeting in London, one of the most accomplished linguists in England, said to me on the public platform: "Don't you mind what people say to you about that word 'pal.' If any one says to you that that word is vulgar he is only showing his own ignorance; for it is a Sanscrit word of good standing; it comes to us from India through the gypsies; and it is as old as any Greek or Latin word you ever read or heard of."

When crossing the Atlantic from America I got into intimate touch with a young Brahman, on his way back to India. He told me that the Sanscrit word pal did not mean chum or companion so much as it meant a friend, or *one who stoops down to do another a good turn.*

A retired Indian Medical Missionary told me, when in Scotland, that the word pal was defined in his Sanscrit dictionary as a keeper, *one who shepherds or looks after another.*

When an organisation has proved itself to be an instrument in God's hand for the salvation of men, professing Christians should not give it the cold shoulder simply because of its name. There are, I suppose, still some people who object to what Samson did to deliver his land from the hand of the Philistines, because the instrument he used had a not very literary name. As far as literary quality goes I may assume that Catch-my-Pal will compare favourably any day with "the jawbone of an ass," at any rate.

In answer to the Scotch minister I may say that the movement whose name so upset him has been going, is going, and will go on without his aid or patronage.

In answer to the bishop I may say the name is not vulgar; it does not savour of the gutter and the corner-boy. But assume for the moment that it does, there are hundreds of men and women and children who can stand up to testify and thank God that the movement of which Catch-my-Pal is the name has already saved many a corner-boy and many a corner-girl OUT of the gutter. That is enough for me, and it should be enough for the bishop.

The bishop, quite unconsciously, gave the movement the highest commendation. There are men and women in the gutters. There are corner boys and corner girls. By all means we must try to save them, and if the name of this society so appeals to them as to win them, will the bishop, as a Christian shepherd, sit upon his dignity and refuse to rejoice that even by a society with such a vulgar name the lost are being sought and saved?

But where some minds grovel among words and scent nothing but vulgarity, other minds penetrate to their spirit and detect their nobility. At one of our great Catch-my-Pal Church Parades on a Sunday afternoon in Armagh Cathedral in 1910, that grand old man of Irish Christendom, Primate Alexander, who had one of the most refined minds and the sweetest literary instincts among the ministers of Christ in the Three Kingdoms, said in his own magnificent manner: "I am glad that this name, Catch-my-Pal, has been given to this movement, because it has got a half playful twang about it which appeals to the popular imagination." With his *imprimatur* on it, I do not much care what anybody may say about the name.

CHAPTER VIII

Sandy and Uncle Sam

MANY friends have sorely strained their vocabularies in trying to improve the name of the crusade.

A Scotch friend started the work in his town, and asked me to address a meeting. On my way to his house from the station I was much amused to find the walls placarded with enormous posters proclaiming that I was to address a meeting of "The Catch-my-Brother Total Abstinence Union"! I stood and looked at each poster and said "Catch-my-Br-r-r-r-ither-r-r-r!"

When sitting at tea with my friend I asked him why he gave such a name to the society.

"Ah, well, ye see we didn't think the name Catch-my-Pal would take over here in Scotland."

"Are there any women in Scotland?" I inquired.

"Oh, yes," said he.

"Are there any women in your town?" said I.

"Oh, yes."

"Will there be any women at the meeting to-night?"

"Oh, yes."

"Well," said I, "if there are women at your meeting to-night, I'll have them into the society. The women are coming into it in scores and hundreds all over Ulster. I suppose you will call their section of the work, 'Catch-my-Sister'? Now, who is going to catch the sister? Will a sister catch a sister? Or will a brother catch a sister? And if it is the brother who is to catch the sister, will you please tell me whose brother is to catch the sister? Besides, if you adopt this plan you must go round the whole gamut of the family relationship, and name each section according to the batch of relations you put into it. One section will be called 'Catch-my-Brother,' and another 'Catch-my-Sister'; another 'Catch-my-Uncle,' and another 'Catch-my-Aunt'; another 'Catch-my-Grandmother,' and another 'Catch-my-Great-Grandmother'; and the most interesting section of all will be the one called 'Catch-my-Mother-in-law!' And in connection with that section the question very naturally crops up, 'And what on earth shall I do with her when I catch her?' "

"Oh, well then," said he, "if that's the way of it, I suppose we had better call it Catch-my-Pal."

So Catch-my-Pal it was; and Catch-my-Pal it is; and Catch-my-Pal it shall be.

Perhaps the most interesting variation I have heard comes from the lips of Uncle Sam. An American gentleman was recently in Belfast. In conversation with a Belfast friend he said, "I guess this is a great Temperance movement you have over here just now. I have heard a great deal about it since I came to your country; and before I go back across the Herring Pond again I guess I'll join these 'Pick-me-Ups' myself."

A short while after the movement started a rector in Lisburn, near Belfast, went to see a young man belonging to his congregation. The young man was not at home, but his mother was there. The rector asked where her son was, and she, forgetting the name Catch-my-Pal, but remembering the two hands on her son's badge, said, "I can't tell you where he is, but I think he has gone down to a meeting of *The Shake-my-Paw Society*."

As long as there is an unreclaimed drunkard in the land there is still a life to be picked up for purity and for God. As long as people go on with the picking up work of Good Samaritanship it does not matter by what name the work is called. As long as there are friendless ones out by life's highways and hedges there is need of the extending of a hand of love from a heart of sympathy. It would be well if there was more of the "Shake-my-Paw" habit in our community. In God's name let no one stand aloof from a movement simply because of its name, if that movement is proving itself successful in picking up God's lost children. It is a matter of indifference to me whether my readers call themselves "Catch-my-Pals" or "Pick-me-Ups," or "Shake-my-Paws," or spurn these names, as long as they catch their fallen brothers and sisters and pick them up for God and Home and Country.

CHAPTER IX

A Rare Party and a Feast of Satisfaction

On the following Monday evening, at nine o'clock, a lady of my congregation came in to speak to me about a forthcoming bazaar. We talked about it for some time, and as I was anxious about the men's coming I was also anxious about the lady's going. I made several suggestions to her in as tactful a way as I could, that it was really time she was going away; but *I could not get her to budge.* She was talking about a bazaar. At twenty-five minutes past nine I heard a knock at my door. I thought the lady would go at last, but *she did not budge.* She was talking about a bazaar. I ran out to the door and found John Elliott on the step. I asked him in, and he said:

"Yir rivirince, what hour did ye say we were to be here?"

"Half-past nine, John."

"All right, yir rivirince, we have our men, we have our men!" As he said this he went backwards towards the door and disappeared. I shut the door and went in to get the lady out. *She would not budge.* She was talking about a bazaar.

I lived through a small eternity during those five minutes. As the post-office clock was nearly opposite my house, the men were punctual to the moment. At half-past nine I heard another knock. I jumped up and ran to the door, forgetting all about the lady and the bazaar. When I opened the door, I found a crowd of men standing round it; so I threw the door wide

30

open and asked them to come in, saying: "This is grand! men, this is simply grand! I'm delighted to see you. This is grand!"

The men walked in in Indian file. When the lady heard the sound of the tread of marching feet in the hall, *she budged,* came to the door of the room, and stood there, while *thirty-one men* wheeled round her into the room and took up positions all around it. There the men stood, and there the lady stood gazing at them.

After all I was glad she had not gone home. Why? Because it was not long till all Armagh heard about the wonderful party his reverence had! For I have heard that if a woman's heels were as quick as her tongue she could catch lightning enough to light the fire in the morning; and I have also heard of a husband who lived on most affectionate terms with his wife, but did not speak to her for five days—because he did not like to interrupt her. I do not believe these things, but I have heard them.

Having said good-night to the lady I returned to the men, and found that some of the biggest boozers and bursters and topers and soakers of the city had been brought in. The bigger the drinker the more applause he got as he came to the end of the table to sign the pledge. All the new men signed amidst a scene of wild hilarity, and I am sure the people passing by on the footpath must have been saying: *"His reverence is having a rare old time of it."* Certainly I had a rare time. I question if any minister ever had a rarer party at his dining-room table than I had that night. There were several men present that night who were the despair of ministers and police alike, and several others who had broken the hearts of their wives and children.

When all had signed, I said: "Men, you are sitting there three on a chair, and you have not room to kneel down. Will you all please stand up and bow your heads and let us pray?" They all rose up, and some reserve men, to the manner born, stood at attention!

At the close of the prayers I saw the tears running down some of the men's cheeks, and I felt that if the Lord Jesus Christ was anywhere in the world He was in my dining-room that night, with the old power "to seek and to save that which was lost," and that He was seeking and saving those men who were there and then coming to the Father by Him. I had such joy in my own bosom, and saw such joy in the faces of the men who brought in those great drinkers, that I could not help thinking, "if this is the sort of joy that Jesus was looking forward to on the other side of the Cross, it is no wonder it was said of Him, 'Who for the joy that was set before Him endured the Cross, despising the shame.'"

When we began to decide how we should conduct our meetings I suggested that someone should propose that all meetings be opened and closed with religious exercises. A young man who had the reputation of being a great drunkard got up (he was under the influence of drink at the time) and said: "Yir rivirince, I propose that all our meetin's be opened with singin' and prayer." That proposition was seconded and passed, and became the pivot on which the movement turned as a religious instrument in social reform. The man who proposed it is not a drinker to-day.

I have enjoyed many good things at my dining-room table, but never did I enjoy such a feast of satisfaction in the very depths of my being as on that wonderful Monday night. The experience and the memory of it I have as my heritage for ever; they are the rejoicing of my heart.

I said to the men: "We can't meet here again. Thank God, this place is too small. We'll meet in the hall beside my church in Gosford Place at a quarter-

past eight o'clock on next Friday evening. Go out
and scour the town and turn up with your men." And
away those men went, helter-skelter, with all the joy
of a batch of boys rushing out to a football match on
a Saturday afternoon!

CHAPTER X

A Bottle of French Polish

SOME of the thirty-one men who came to me on the third night of the crusade had very remarkable histories of debauch. One of them gave me more insight into the character of the men I was dealing with than any other man I met in Armagh. For some years I had been trying to get him to give up drinking, but without success. As far as I could see there was no way for him to get out into a sober life. In the course of a conversation with him two years after he signed the pledge, he said: "Four days after I signed yir pledge, yir rivirince, I wint to a public house to help the publican to blend whiskies. Ye see I'm a gineral handy man, an' make my livin' by takin' a turn at ennything. Some ov the fellas tould me not to go, as I cuddent kape the pledge I had tuk. But I wint, an' I helped to blend wan hunner an' twinty gallons, yir rivirince, an' I niver touched a drap ov it. An' I have nivir touched a drap since, yir rivirince, by the grace of God. I pray to the Lord Jesus Christ to help me, an' He does help me. An' ye know what soort of a characthur I wuz before I tuk yir pledge. Why, yir rivirince, I wuz in jail wi' drink, an' I wuz in the workhouse wi' drink, an' I wuz in the asylum wi' drink, an' I wuz in the gutthers fur years wi' drink, an' there wuz wan night I wuz that dhrunk I diddint know what I wuz doin'. An' d'ye know what I did do, yir rivirince?"

"No," said I.

"Well, I swallied a whole bottle ov French pollis

34

and mithilated spirits, yir rivirince, an' I wuz very bad."

"I'm sure you were," said I.

"I wuz that," said he. "Ye know where I live, yir rivirince?"

"I do," said I.

"Well, yir rivirince, I wuz that bad that two chaps come to take me up to the infermary on the tap ov the hill, an' d'ye know, I wuz that bad I fell dead sivin times between my own house an' the infermary. It's a fact, yir rivirince, I fell dead sivin times. An' when the fellas got me to the infermary, the docthur, he puts me on the operaytin' table; an' there wuz nurses there, an' the maythrun wuz there, an' the docthur wuz there, an' I wuz there, an' we wur all there. The docthur, he begins to operate with a stomach pump; an' I dunno what happened, yir rivirince, but, by the hokey, part ov the pump disappayred, an' naythur the docthur, nor the maythrun, nor the nurses, nor mesilf, yir rivirince, has ivir seen hilt or hair ov it since! Wan day I wuz lyin' in the bed in the ward, an' a nurse comes over to me, an' sez she:

" 'George.'

" 'Yis,' sez I.

" 'Ye wur bad,' sez she.

" 'Wuz I?' sez I.

" 'Ye wur,' sez she.

" 'An' how bad wuz I?' sez I.

" 'Oh, ye wur very bad,' sez she.

" 'I wuz very bad, wuz I?' sez I.

" 'Ye wur that,' sez she.

" 'An' if I wuz very bad,' sez I, 'how bad wuz I?' sez I.

" 'Ye wur very, very bad,' sez she.

" 'But, how bad wuz I, if I wuz very, very bad?' sez I.

" 'Well, we thought ye wur goin' to die,' sez she.

" 'Ye thought I wuz goin' to die, did ye?' sez I.

35

" 'We did,' sez she.

" 'But I diddint die, did I?' sez I.

" 'No, ye diddint,' sez she.

" 'An' why diddint I die?' sez I.

" 'Because ye wur too full ov spirits,' sez she.

"An,' yir rivirince, I am too full ov spirits to go back to my ould way ov livin'. Thank God, He has made a man ov me. No more intoxicatin' spirits fur me!"

After four years this good man, George Young, is still renewing his youth as a staunch abstainer, a miracle in the streets of the city.

CHAPTER XI

"WE WILL SEE THIS THING THROUGH"

ON the following Friday at a quarter-past eight o'clock *one hundred and five men* walked into the church hall. Sixty-seven new men signed the pledge that night, and among these were some of the biggest drinkers in the city. The scene was most hilarious as these men came forward to put down their names.

When the signing was finished I asked the whole company to rise to their feet. They all stood up, and I told them I was going to ask them to hold up their hands while they repeated the pledge in unison. I explained to them that the uplifted hand was the outward token of the uplifted, prayerful heart. With their right hands uplifted in appeal to Almighty God, one hundred and five men repeated, phrase by phrase after me, the following pledge:

"For God and Home and Native Land, I promise, by God's help, to abstain from all intoxicating drinks as beverages, and to do all that in me lies to promote the cause of total abstinence by getting others to join the Union."

I did not intend to ask the men to do anything more than to repeat the pledge, but when I saw all the hands up I said: "Men, shut your fists!" What I was going to ask them to do the next moment I had no more idea of than I had of what was going to happen at two and a half minutes past one o'clock the next afternoon. But suddenly the watchword, *"We will see this thing through!"* came into my mind, and I asked the men to repeat it word by word after me. I told them that the

37

closed fist was the symbol of Irish Christian determination; and, with closed fists uplifted, the company said word by word after me, with great deliberation:

WE—WILL—SEE—THIS—THING—
THROUGH!

Having called for three cheers for total abstinence in our city, which were given with whole-hearted Irish enthusiasm, I asked the men to bow their heads while we prayed. I led in a prayer in general terms, and then I asked them all to repeat with me the Lord's Prayer.

One of the most delightful experiences I have ever had, as a minister of the Gospel, was hearing many men there that night who hardly ever once entered a church, and some men who, judging by their outward lives, probably never uttered a prayer at their bedsides from their hearts to the heart of the Eternal Father, saying after me, "Our Father Who art in heaven, hallowed be Thy name, Thy kingdom come, Thy will be done in earth as it is in heaven."

We proceeded to organise ourselves. It was proposed that we should hold monthly meetings, but I objected to this proposal. Our enthusiasm was intense, and I thought it would be *fatal to wait a month* before we had another meeting. I said that our enthusiasm needed continual fuelling, and that it was necessary to hold a weekly meeting for recruiting purposes. It was agreed to hold weekly meetings, to have no set temperance speeches, but that anyone might speak who so desired, to devote most of our time to the enrolment of new members and devising means for gathering in all who were in any way addicted to drink.

I asked that the pledge and watchword should be repeated at the close of every meeting, and it was so decided. I know that some people think this is a mistake, as the frequent repetition is likely to degenerate into a mere formality. But nothing succeeds like success. Besides, this practice of taking a vow at the close of our meetings has an ancient Christian sanction. Pliny the Younger, Governor of Bithynia, laid certain charges against the Christians, and he wrote to the Emperor, Trajan, in 97 A. D., stating how he investigated these charges. He says, "They," (that is the Christians) "declare that all their guilt or error amounted to was this; they met on certain mornings before daybreak and sang one after another hymn to Christ as God, at the same time binding themselves by oath not to commit any crime, but to abstain from theft, robbery, adultery, perjury, or repudiation of trust; after this was done the meeting broke up." If the early Church adopted such a method of dealing with the common sins of the times, our Union cannot be very far astray in asking its members to hold up their hands, not to take an oath, but to appeal to God for help to keep their pledges, and to shut their hands in token of Christian determination while they say they will see this thing through.

We appointed some office-bearers. As President we chose Dr. Robert Gray, F.R.C.P.I., an enthusiast in total abstinence work. And in these days, when the medical profession is so magnificently identifying itself with the total abstinence propaganda, it is significant that the first president of the first branch of the newest Total Abstinence Society in the country is a medical man. We appointed some vice-presidents, and a committee. Among our officers were some of the well-known drinkers of Armagh. The public meeting was held every Friday and the committee meeting every Monday, and *it was quite delightful to find men sitting on the committee devising means of saving the city from the curse with which they themselves had formerly helped to curse the city.*

The public meetings became the talk of the city and neighbourhood, as, for some months, great drinkers were being enrolled at every one of them. Several "schools" of drinkers that used to meet in various saloons began to be broken up, their members joining the Catch-my-Pal Union. The members of one notorious "school" that met in a certain saloon began to "catch" one another for total abstinence; and every night when, at pledging time, one of these men was seen coming forward with a pal, there was great applause. It became known that all of this school were caught except one who held back for a long time. On the night he was caught the meeting was almost frantic as he walked up to take the pledge before the president. The men became surprised at their own success in "catching men," and sometimes during the week the word would go round that a notorious drinker was caught and would appear at the next meeting, when he would get such a reception as was enough to make him feel that, whatever fellowship he used to have in the saloon, this outburst was brotherhood indeed.

CHAPTER XII

"The Button Men"

At our second meeting in Gosford Place School we decided to adopt, as our Badge, a button with clasped hands across it, and the words, "Protestant Total Abstinence Union" around it. Some time afterwards we added another button with the words, "Catch-my-Pal Total Abstinence Union."

The buttons became so popular in the city and neighbourhood that the phrase "taking the pledge" dropped out of use. Those who joined the Union were said to "take the button," and those who broke the pledge were said to "break the button." As men only had been introduced to the Union up till now, the members were known as "The Button Men."

The reform wrought by "the button" soon became very apparent. Several districts of the city that used to be characterised by brawling on Saturday nights were almost completely changed. Saloons were almost emptied. Bakers, drapers, fruiterers, and grocers began to reap the harvest through the diverting of money from the saloons. It was said there was hardly a fritter of a beefsteak left on the benches of the butchers on Saturday nights. They sold meat instead of bones! There were more children's boots sold in the winter, 1909-1910, than in any similar period within living memory. Many merchants told me that debts which they looked on as bad debts, owed by the men who had been drinkers, were paid up to the very last farthing. Men began to go to church who seldom or never went to church before. The first Catch-my-Pal

THE HAPPY ART OF CATCHING MEN

Church Parade was held one Sunday afternoon in my church, which has six hundred sittings. As many men as packed the church marched two deep through the streets. There was a city sensation! As they entered the church, they received special hymn sheets from four men who had been among the heaviest drinkers in the city; and something of *a church sensation* was caused when other men who had been drinkers walked into the aisles and took up the collection! Would God we had more such church sensations!

I began to realise how great was the work being done when I found that many a woman whom I did not know met me on the street, stopped me, shook my hand, and, with tears in her eyes, said: "Yir rivirince, thank God for the Catch-my-Pal, for I hardly ever knew what it was to be happy till my husband signed your pledge." I have seen more gratitude in women's eyes since July, 1909, than I saw during the whole of my ministry of seventeen years before that.

An Armagh lady was going to live in Dublin, and had been in the capital for some time while looking for a house. When she returned she engaged a furniture remover, who sent her a man to pack her glass and china. When he arrived she refused to let him do her packing, as he was such a drinker. He told her what had been going on in the city during her absence, and how he and so many other drinkers had become new men, and that no man could pack her things better than himself. "Why, ma'am," said he, "whole streets are changed. Many of us never had a bit of bacon except on Christmas Day; and many a man of us had it only on a Christmas now and then; but, I declare, ma'am, if you walked down ——— Street any day now at half-past one o'clock, you'd hear the bacon sizzlin' in the pans in every house in the street." The man was allowed to pack the china, and the lady told me afterwards that not a piece of it was broken.

The success of the Union seized on the imagination

42

of the community. A teacher in a school about two miles from the city asked a class of junior pupils to write an essay on "Armagh." The essay of one pupil was as follows: "Armagh is a very old city. It is famous for its two cathedrals and its temperance society."

A great fire occurred one morning about three o'clock in a motor garage near my Manse. I was wakened by the crackling of glass, and I rushed to the police station and got the constabulary out. Later on I was standing beside a man who was manipulating the hose. It was found there was little pressure of water.

"How is it," I asked him, "that there is not enough supply to meet an emergency like this?"

"How could you expect water to be in the Armagh pipes now, yir rivirince?"

"And why not?"

"Why, *your teetotallers have drunk it all!*"

The lamp-post at which I found the first six men became known as "The Teetotal Lamp," and it was supposed by some that there was virtue in it! It was reported that some men who were becoming weak in their resolutions leaned against it to receive fresh courage! One day I was talking to a pal beside the lamp-post. We saw a man, a little under the influence of drink, leaning against a telephone pole about ten yards away. My pal shouted to him: "What's the use in leanin' aginst a thing like that? Shure, it will do you no good! If you want to get straightened up, come over here, man, and lean agin the lamp-post!" That same pal met me on another day beside the lamp-post. He had a mighty record as a drinker and a wit. He stopped me, lowered his left eyebrow, and, with a merry twinkle in his eye, said, as he pointed to the lamp-post: "D'ye know, yir rivirince, d'ye know, there's a whole lot of fellas in Armagh who haven't taken the button yit, and they're afraid ov their lives to go near that lamp-post, for fear they'd catch the infecshun!"

CHAPTER XIII

Catching the "Infecshun"

The "infecshun" was soon caught by other towns. Six men in the village of Milford, a centre of the linen industry about two miles from Armagh, gathered around one of the village lamp-posts. They decided to start the movement among their pals, and resorted to the house of an elder of my congregation, where they signed the pledge in one another's presence. They went out to catch the village, and it was thought that, in some respects, Milford outstripped Armagh in its newly found zeal. Indeed the movement had its greatest success all over the country in manufacturing centres where men walked in crowds to and from their work. These times of going to and fro were discovered to be splendid recruiting seasons. When a number of men in any factory "took the button" and began to work, it was not long till it was said that the non-buttoned man "hadn't the life of a dog of it" till he took the button too. In Milford, as in Armagh, men were enrolled who had never before gone near a temperance meeting, and lives were changed which had been looked upon as "far gone" indeed.

When I saw and heard of the changed lives in Armagh and Milford *I decided to extend the movement over the country,* and I became rather impatient in my congregational work. One Sunday after the evening service I said to my wife, "I must go off to-morrow and see if I can get this thing started in some other places." I had not thought of any places in par-

44

ticular, so, on the following morning, I started on my motor bicycle, with my wife in a side-car, to find new opportunities for Catch-my-Pal. We went to Richhill, Tandragee and Portadown. Each town would receive the new idea, and, as I came home, I thought I had done a good day's pioneer work. The Milford pals thought the same for they made the rafters ring with their cheers when I addressed them that night and told them of my mission.

That night I saw the Ulster heather take fire.

On the following Friday we decided at our meeting in Armagh that we would storm Portadown on Saturday night with the Armagh Pal Artillery. It was agreed to send a jaunting car with the storming party and to pay the hire out of the funds. We asked for six volunteers to "man" the car with me. We arranged to start from the lamp-post, that we might bring the "infecshun" from it to Portadown. The news of the storming party and their plan of campaign went quickly round the city and neighbourhood. A large crowd gathered round the lamp-post on Saturday evening to see us off. We began our advance on Portadown amid the cheers of the crowd, and I found that a second car with six men was coming after us. Where did this car, with its six men, come from? And who were they? They were six of the men of "the right sort," who hired a car at their own expense to come and help us in the Portadown adventure. In this campaign we are said to capture men of "the right sort" when we bring in the biggest drinkers.

On arrival at Portadown we went to a hall and tried an indoor meeting which proved a failure, though I had sent about two thousand circulars ahead for distribution among the men coming out of the factories. *We decided to go to the street.* Some deal boxes were commandeered from the front of a draper's shop and were formed into a platform at a lamp-post. A great crowd assembled, and, when I had told my

45

story of the work in Armagh and Milford, I asked the twelve men of Armagh to come up on the boxes. They did not know I was going to ask them up, but they all responded to my call and stood up before the gaze of that Portadown throng as living object lessons. The splendid action of the twelve had an instantaneous effect which drove home my appeal as nothing else could have done.

I asked all who wished to do for their town what the men of Armagh had done for theirs to come with us to the hall, in which our meeting failed an hour before. At our second meeting there was no failure. *Seventy-nine* men signed the pledge, and undertook to go and catch their pals. This was the first draught in waters away from the immediate vicinity of Armagh. It was inspiring! It made one feel that the "wonderful thing" *was* happening!

One of the men who signed that night pawned his clothes before the meeting on the street. The first thing he did after the meeting in the hall was to redeem his clothes and go down the street, a proud man, with his bundle under his arm.

He had two suits. He was not like the man in the story. It was at an auction; a trunk was put up for sale. The auctioneer said:

"Paddy, why don't you buy the trunk?"

"Arrah, sur, an' what wud Oi do wid a trunk?"

"Put your clothes in it, of course."

"Hoogh! an' me go naked?"

On the following Saturday night I went again to Portadown and addressed another crowd at the lamp, which became the "teetotal lamp" of that town. Another fine contingent joined our ranks, and the campaign was well established on the banks of the Bann.

I went to Lurgan on the next Saturday night and addressed a crowd around a lamp-post, now known as the "teetotal lamp" of Lurgan. One of the merchants of that town told me that some of the saloon-keepers were thinking of enlarging their premises, as their bars were so thronged, especially on Saturday nights. I saw the bars thronged on that night and I was, perhaps, over-zealous when I stood on the box by the lamp and said, "I have come here to-night, in the name of the Lord God Almighty, that a blow may be given to the drink trade in your town this very night." But the facts are: I knew what was being done in Armagh; and that what was done in one place could be done in another; I felt God Almighty *was* in the movement; what was done in Armagh was done with even greater success in Lurgan, for, in the course of a few weeks about two thousand members joined the Union; and no saloon-keeper spoke of enlarging his premises after that night.

At one of the weekly meetings a pal gave this testimony: "I was a constant drinker. One Saturday night I went into a pub to drink. I found no one there but the bar-man. I went to another pub and found no one but the bar-man. I went to a third pub and found no one but the bar-man. So, when I saw how things were going, I said to myself, 'The game's up with me too,' and I came that night to the Pal meeting in the town hall where I saw the fellows I expected to find in the pubs. And, as the game was up, I signed the pledge and took the button."

It is wonderful how God often uses very mean instruments in bringing salvation to men. "A face as long as a Lurgan spade," is one of the proverbs of Ulster. The first night I spoke on the Lurgan street I said, "I have often heard of a Lurgan spade. Did any of you ever hear of a Lurgan mug? Is there a Lurgan mug here to-night—a man who is going to the Devil through drink, who might be going to God if he would only give the drink up?" We must become all things to all men that we may gain some. I was led that night to venture on that slang expression. But it gained at least one man who told me months afterwards, "When you said, 'Is there a Lurgan mug here?' I said to myself, 'I am a Lurgan mug'; and I went home and went down on my knees and confessed my sin; and I rose up, having made up my mind that, with the help of God, I'd be a Lurgan mug no more." And now, after more than two years, he can stand four square to all the town as one of the most respected and trusted men that walk its streets.

On the first Sunday of 1910, I preached at the first church parade of the Lurgan Branch. Eleven hundred men marched in a solemn procession through the streets to the church, and it was said that a saloon-keeper who usually "took" about $250 a week acknowledged that, on the Friday after the parade, only sixty cents were taken over the counter!

CHAPTER XIV

The Publicans' Prayer for the Priest and the Parson

Father Sheerin was promoted from the position of curate in Armagh to that of parish priest in Crossmaglen. Some weeks after he left Armagh I met a Roman Catholic saloon-keeper in the street. He said:

"Good evening, your reverence."

"Good evening," said I.

"Trade's very slack just now, your reverence."

"Is it?" said I.

"It is," said he.

"Do you help your own trade?" said I.

"What do you mean?" said he.

"Are you a customer of your own?" said I.

"What do you mean?" said he.

"I mean, do you take any drink yourself?" said I.

"Oh, no," said he.

"Do you allow your barman to take drink?" said I.

"Oh, no, not if I know it," said he.

"Is it not so that you, men who are in the trade, exact a pledge of total abstinence from your barmen?" said I.

"Yes, if we can manage it," said he.

"Then you want total abstinence on *your* side of the counter?" said I.

"Certainly," said he.

"Well, you see," said I, "*I* want total abstinence on *my* side of the counter, and that is why I am going on with the Catch-my-Pal work."

"Well, your reverence," said he, "we all prayed

49

earnestly that Father Sheerin might get a parish of his own as far from Armagh as he could go; and our prayers were heard, and he's gone! And now, your reverence, we are all praying that *you* may get a call somewhere out of Armagh, as far as you can go, and we believe you'll go too!"

I cannot say that the call came in answer to the publicans' prayer; but it did come. Indeed it seemed as if I wrote it myself in a letter I sent to various Irish newspapers, as I thought the time had come to let the world know what was being done in Armagh and its neighbourhood. The Rev. Samuel Prenter, D.D., Ex-Moderator of the Irish General Assembly, wrote an article on my letter. He spoke of "The New Reformation" which had begun to dawn in Armagh. Judging by the subsequent history of the movement, he showed really remarkable foresight as to its possibilities. He said the letter was being talked about everywhere; and I soon discovered how true this was, for, within a week, I was deluged with letters from all over the United Kingdom. I required a postman nearly all for myself every morning. Requests for information came from every country in Europe except Turkey and Portugal. Afterwards I had requests for information from all over the United States and Canada, and almost every British Dominion beyond the seas. Similar requests came from China and Japan. I felt it was quite impossible for me to settle down to my work as a parish minister. The "call" to leave Armagh had surely come! And I thought of the publican's prayer!

I venture to affirm that no church in the United Kingdom has taken a more definite stand on the drink question than the Irish Presbyterian Church, and no man has helped more to that end than the Rev. John Macmillan, D.D., the convener of the Temperance Committee, who, in the following year, in recognition of his service to the cause of Temperance, was appointed Moderator of the Church. He consulted his committee about the Catch-my-Pal crusade, and wrote to tell me that the Committee desired me to conduct a three months' campaign over the country, while they would supply my church in Armagh. I agreed to do as desired, and my congregation nobly consented. When the three months were ended Dr. Macmillan made a similar arrangement for another three. When the second period ended, another arrangement was made for a third, and I was in a fix. I was being weaned away from my congregation, and my congregation was being weaned away from me. I saw that I must either give up this work or my congregation. I have no private means and I did not marry for money. A committee was formed to look after the interests of the movement throughout the country, but they were in no position to offer me a salary. One day I said to my wife, "What shall I do? I have no way of supporting you and the boys, and I have no guarantee that things will work out right if I resign my congregation and my salary and Manse." She had more faith than I had; and it is only fair to her to say that I made a venture, more on my wife's faith than on my own. For she said, "There is only one thing for you to do. Give up your congregation. God has made so many other firesides happy through this movement, we may be sure He will not forsake our fireside. Certainly give up your church." I said, "All right, then, that settles it. I'll resign at the next meeting of the Presbytery." So, at the next meeting, I resigned. Many said to me that I was "a born fool" to do anything of the kind. But after four years I have yet to find wherein my folly lay. I question if there is any minister in the world who has seen more immediate fruit of his ministry than I have been privileged to see in the hundreds of homes that have been made happy and men and women and children who have been lifted up out of the gutters of drunken debauchery. I shall ever keep in grateful memory the kind indulgence given to me by my congregation during the year I was being weaned from them before my actual resignation.

I was supported by the General Assembly's Committee for nine months after my resignation of my ministry in Armagh, and I can never forget how the church of my fathers stood by me and mothered me in the infancy of my larger ministry. Since April, 1911, I have had a salary from the Executive Committee of the Catch-my-Pal movement.

CHAPTER XV

How the Cause Sped on Its Way

At a meeting of the General Assembly of the Irish Presbyterian Church, held in Belfast in October, 1909, I was permitted to make a statement about the work in Armagh and neighbouring towns. All day I was wondering what I should say at the evening meeting. I had told the story in the public Press in the letter already referred to, and I did not wish to repeat it. I asked a minister what I ought to do, and he said, "Tell your story." "But," I said, "you have all read it in the Press, and you know all I have to say. I cannot concoct facts." "Oh, yes, you can," he answered! I tried to prepare a speech, and I worried over it all day, but I could put down nothing that satisfied me, and I found, notwithstanding what the brother said, that I could not concoct facts. I was booked for a speech, and I was beginning to wish I had not asked permission to speak. I was a bundle of nerves when the Moderator called on me to address the house. My address seemed to make a profound impression. I can say this without any egotism, as I felt, when I had finished, that I hardly knew what I had been saying. So deep was the impression that the Moderator asked the Assembly to unite in singing, as an expression of thanksgiving, part of the sixty-eighth Psalm:

> "O God, Thou to Thine heritage
> Didst send a plenteous rain,
> Whereby Thou, when it weary was,
> Didst it refresh again.

"The Lord Himself did give the word,
    The word abroad did spread;
Great was the company of them
    The same who published.

"Kings of great armies foiled were,
    And forced to flee away;
And women, who remained at home,
    Distributed the prey.

"Though ye have lain among the pots,
    Like doves ye shall appear,
Whose wings with silver, and with gold
    Whose feathers covered are."

The Assembly then engaged in solemn prayer for a blessing on the work begun in the old ecclesiastical capital of our native land.

After that address I was surprised at the way my brethren in the Irish ministry took up the work and upheld my hands wherever I went on my mission.

A horse was being driven in a dray along a street in New York. He was a jibber. As they say in Scotland—he took the sturdies; or, as we say in Ireland—he rusted. Many attempts were made by his driver and by passers-by to make him move, but he stolidly stood his ground. When he was about to be despaired of a gentleman came along the street. He took in the situation. It was in the time of the snow. The gentleman lifted a handful of snow and rubbed it over the horse's nose. Immediately the horse went on. The driver asked the gentleman:

"What did you do to that horse? We have been trying for some time to get him to move but he would not budge. What did you do to that horse?"

The gentleman answered:

"Oh, I guess it was very simple. The horse was run down in his ideas. *He simply needed a new idea.* That was all."

It seemed as if some of the temperance work of the

country had come to a standstill. It simply needed a new idea.

I was going to Derry one day in a train with several other ministers. One of them said to me: "This Catch-my-Pal is such a simple thing, it's a wonder none of us ever thought of it before." I said: "The time was when mothers all over the country were greatly bothered by the pins that stuck into the sides of their infant children. The whole peace of families was upset by stray pins. The safety pin was invented. One day a mother showed a safety pin to the assembled family. They all examined it and handed it back to the mother. She held it in her hand and expressed the family's opinion when she said: "Dear me, that is *such a simple thing*, isn't it a wonder none of us ever thought of it before?"

If the people had not been taught on the temperance question the Catch-my-Pal movement could not have been. If the movement did not bring any new material to the temperance pile perhaps it touched that pile with a new fire. When I went out on my mission people found I had nothing new to say on the question. It seemed to me that they had heard nearly everything that could be said on it, but that it needed to be presented in a new light. *All I did was to tell my story and lay stress on Good Samaritanship.* The engine of temperance reform was filled with material for fire. The fire was somewhat dull. A live coal from off the altar of the Lord was put into the pile on July 13th, 1909, and the engine sped on its way.

I addressed a meeting, and oftentimes two meetings, every night in the week, and usually two every Sunday. I slept in a different bed every night, but I did not sleep long. I had no secretary; I was amongst strangers all the day except when I was in trains, when I tried to be alone; and, when my kind hosts thought I was in my bed, I was sitting in my bedroom till

55

three or four o'clock every morning writing letters to all parts of the world.

And here I desire to record my profound gratitude to God for all His goodness to me in giving me such health and resolution as enabled me to get through an amount of work which I never could have imagined myself capable of accomplishing.

Everywhere I went my story created the greatest interest and enthusiasm. In places where temperance sentiment was weak I found my story made it strong. Men and women thronged around the Catch-my-Pal standard, eager to be found in the van of a crusade fighting for the formation of a better public opinion. Sometimes whole audiences would sign the pledge and repeat the watchword. Men and women came to the meetings with no intention of signing, and before they went away they found, to their own surprise, that they had "taken the button."

When I held an inaugural meeting I usually did not leave the platform till it was arranged when and where the next meeting would be held, *for I did not consider there was much use in getting a number of people to come and sign, if they were to go off again at the close of the meeting as so many unrelated atoms, never to meet again. My endeavour was to leave an organisation behind me in every place I visited—an organisation for recruiting purposes, an organisation of workers.*

A card was given to each person entering a meeting, and when I had made my appeal I asked all who wished to sign the cards to put their names down. When the cards were signed I asked all who had signed them to come up to the front and hand their cards to me. When I had them at the front I kept them there till they had repeated the pledge with uplifted hands and shut their fists and said, "We will see this thing through."

CATCH-MY-PAL CRUSADE

WORKER'S PLEDGE

Let every man and every woman willing to

DO

something to save our land from drink, sign the pledge on this card.

"For God and Home and Native Land, I promise, by God's help, to abstain from all intoxicating drinks as beverages, and to do all that in me lies to promote the Cause of Total Abstinence by getting at least one drinker to sign the pledge and join the Anti-Drink Crusade."

BEFORE YOU SIGN, ASK YOURSELF THREE QUESTIONS:
1.—Did I LIFT UP a fallen one during the past year?
2.—Did I TRY to lift up a fallen one during the past year?
3.—Did I PRAY that I might be able to lift up a fallen one during the past year?

Even though you are already a Total Abstainer, sign this pledge and become a

WORKER

Name ....

Address ....

Congregation ....

WE-WILL-SEE-THIS-THING-THROUGH!

In one town eighty-four men were at the meeting. Every man took the pledge that night. But these eighty-four were nearly all total abstainers, and, on the following day, the publicans were amused to hear that so many total abstainers had taken the pledge. They laughed at the Catch-my-Pal movement, and thought that not much evil would come to their trade. But they laughed too soon.

It was arranged when and where the eighty-four were to meet the next week. At the second meeting these eighty-four brought in eighty-seven, many of whom were drinkers; and before the next weekly meeting, when one hundred and twenty more were brought in, some saloon men of the meaner sort in that town were offering free drinks and free suppers to any men who would come into their bars with the Catch-my-Pal buttons in their coats. Seven hundred and two men were enrolled in that small town in seven weeks.

In another town I was told by a minister, when going to the meeting, that Catch-my-Pal "would not take" there. On entering the hall I saw it packed with about five hundred people. I told them I had heard the movement would not "take" with them, as they were "a peculiar people," but that I would not leave the platform till three-fourths of them had signed the pledge! Three hundred and sixty of them signed. The movement did "take" and, on the testimony of many witnesses, it revolutionised the district in its relation to the drinking habit.

Five weeks before one of my meetings in a town in County Down, a merchant met me at a railway junction and told me the saloon-keepers of the town were in dread of the coming meeting. I laughed at my friend, but he said it was really so. And, indeed, it was so. On the night of the meeting I addressed not one but two assemblies, attended by men who came in their working clothes. Five hundred of them "took the button." The greatest enthusiasm prevailed. Five hundred apostles of total abstinence were at work in the town and neighbourhood the following day, and the publicans' dread was more than justified.

Shortly before Christmas, 1909, I went through a severe snow-storm to a little town which had the worst reputation for drink in its county. The local school-master told me at the meeting that ninety per cent. of the men in the town were drinkers. I asked the meeting if this was so, and the meeting agreed with the master. There were one hundred and seven persons present. I did not think there would be any response to my appeal so soon before Christmas, as I supposed

that in such a place the men would not so bind themselves as to forego their usual Christmas bout. To my
surprise, over eighty "took the button." I congratulated the men on their action, and said that as their
town was in a hollow and was then covered with snow,
I might, if they would keep their pledge, congratulate
myself on being like Benaiah, the son of Jehoiada, who
went into a pit in the time of the snow and slew a lion.
It is now acknowledged that from that night *a new
chapter in the life of the town* began to be written.
The majority of those who signed kept their pledges.
Several of the most abandoned drinkers are on their
feet again, and men who were on the verge of bank-
ruptcy are now prospering in business.

In the heat of the General Election on January,
1910, I went to a small town in another county. When
on my way past the corner of the town square to the
place of meeting I walked into a crowd of about twenty men, many of whom were under the influence of
drink. I asked them to come to the meeting, but they
refused. I told them I would tell them some good
stories, but they were not to be caught. When I was
introduced to the meeting in the hall I said I thought
it would be a good thing if we all went out and tried
to get the fellows in from the corner of the square.
I asked all who would like to help me to come out with
me. Every man in the hall came out into the square.
I asked them to form four deep, and as they did not
seem to heed me I said to the rector, who had been in
the chair:

"Rector, will *you* get them to form four deep?"

And the rector, a true son of Connaught, shouted:

"Form *four* deep every *one* of you!"

Every one of us formed four deep, and we marched
towards the men at the corner. As we approached the
corner I turned and said to the men in the procession:
"Get into open order. Spread yourselves out and
march right into these fellows and mix yourselves up

with them. When we are all well mixed up with them we'll form again and march for the hall!" We walked into them, and when we were well mixed up with them I shouted: "Now, boys, for the hall!" We marched back to the hall and swept in the boys from the corner. I was told that nearly every one of them signed the pledge that night. One of them was so drunk he did not know he had signed. The next morning a pal called to see him, and reminded him of the meeting of the previous night.

"But I was at no meetin' last night."

"Oh, yes, you were at the Catch-my-Pal meetin'."

"Me at the Catch-my-Pal meetin' last night!"

"Yes, an' you signed the pledge too."

"What! *Me* signed the pledge?"

"Yes, you signed the pledge last night."

"Well, if I signed the pledge, I'll keep it."

And he did keep it. I addressed a meeting in that town fifteen months after that night. A local magistrate presented a silver medal to the pal who proved himself the best worker in the branch, and I was asked to hand the medal to the man who came up for it. The man who came up was the man who had been so far down that he did not know what he was doing when he signed the pledge! And now, after four years, he is one of the most successful and happy and respected men in the town.

At the close of a meeting I addressed in a town in County Antrim, the chairman, a magistrate and one of the most active workers in every good cause, said to me: "I have been working for temperance for over thirty years, and that is the best temperance meeting I have ever been at. The men we want to get to temperance meetings were here to-night. I never saw them at a temperance meeting before." Nearly all the drinkers in the town were present.

Reports of these meetings were published all over the country. I was quite unable to respond to all the calls that came to me for meetings. I arranged to hold nearly all my first meetings in towns of strategic importance, and asked all branches started in them to do their utmost for their own towns and then to go out along the lines of missionary effort to the neighbouring villages. Many men and women started the work among themselves in many centres. One branch, which I did not visit till six months after it was started, had over a thousand members on the roll, though there were only nine hundred persons in the town!

There was, perhaps, no place where more enthusiasm was shown than in the City of Derry. If her walls would not surrender to King James she opened wide her gates to the Catch-my-Pal army. Two battalions of the army entrenched themselves at Ebrington and at Clooney on "The Waterside." The men of the city proper said, "God is come into the camp at Waterside," for they heard how women's hearts were being healed and children's lives gladdened through the fight the Catch-my-Pal men were making with the drink. So signal was the success of the Waterside men, they determined to storm the city itself. They marched out in battle array in two brigades. They crossed the bridge unopposed. The city opened her gates, while the citizens, with the bishop at their head, turned out to meet them. A great meeting of welcome was held in one of the Presbyterian Churches, and, for the first time since the siege, an Episcopal bishop went into a Presbyterian pulpit, and met such a volley of Catch-my-Pal enthusiasm as must have pierced his heart through with the desire to occupy many a Presbyterian pulpit again!

After that meeting all the Derry churches, including the Cathedral, opened their doors to the movement, and a branch was started in connection with every congregation. At an open-air demonstration held in Derry in 1911, the local secretary of the National Society for the Prevention of Cruelty to Children stated on the platform that, since the starting of the Catch-my-Pal movement in that district in 1909, *the cases of cruelty to children had been reduced by fifty per cent.*

I was asked to address the Annual Meeting of The Society of Friends in Dublin. I never had a more interesting experience than at that meeting. There was a charm about it I found nowhere else. I was allowed twenty-five minutes, and when I had spoken about ten minutes there were some expressions of appreciation. After five minutes more there was faint applause. A little later the applause was more pronounced, and, as I closed, the applause was almost unrestrained. It was proposed, seconded, and decided, to form a Friends' Branch of the Union. I then administered the pledge. Most of the Friends stood up, held up their hands, repeated the pledge, shut their fists, and said, "We will see this thing through." A gentleman afterwards said to me: "I have been at Friends' meetings all my life, and I never heard applause at one of them before, and, of course, I never saw us rise and shut our fists as we did to-day!"

The movement spread over Ireland from Culdaff to Cork, and from Donaghadee to Dromore West. There are about three thousand Protestants in Limerick city. Almost one third of them were at the meeting I' addressed there. The minister of a Presbyterian church in a town in the South told me that every Protestant in the district "took the button."

Many Roman Catholics came to my meetings in all parts of the country. There were four of them at one meeting. They went and caught their pals and brought them to the next meeting. They multiplied till there were sixty-four coming to the Protestant Total Abstinence Union. The local secretary wrote to ask me what they should do with the Roman Catholic members. I replied that it would be best to give them over to their priest. This was done, and the result was a race between Roman Catholics and Protestants such as was seen in Armagh. They vied with one another in saving their town from their common curse.

About 140,000 men and women joined the Union during the first year in Ireland; and almost 500 branches were formed in less than two years.

CHAPTER XVI

The Sound of the Tread of Marching Feet

As the chief end of the Catch-my-Pal movement is to form a well defined public opinion against the drinking customs of our time and in favour of legislation that will abolish the facilities for drinking, we have, from the beginning of the crusade, held great Church Parades and open-air Demonstrations.

Men and women of all classes of society have been willing to come out in procession along our streets and to march to church. The services are usually conducted by the several ministers of the various Protestant churches taking part together. It seemed as if a veritable ecclesiastical miracle was wrought by the movement, as it became quite customary to see Episcopalian, Presbyterian, Methodist, and Congregational ministers taking part in the one service. I preached in an Episcopal church one evening. The rector read the prayers. One Presbyterian minister read the first lesson, and another read the second. A Presbyterian minister gave out the hymns, and a Presbyterian minister sang a solo to the organ accompaniment.

These parades have been the means of bringing to church men and women who had almost forgotten the way to the House of God. Some people who have absented themselves for a long time from church do not care to be seen coming to it again. They fear the criticism of their neighbours. But they will come if there is a crowd in which they can hide themselves; and after they have come in the crowd they make bold to come alone. Almost one of the first signs of the changed life of those who have given up the drink in the course of this crusade has been the purchase of new clothes and attendance at public worship.

The Protestant Churches of Ireland have been brought nearer to one another by the Catch-my-Pal movement than by any other movement of our times. And the church parades have manifested the spirit of unity in a way that nothing else could do.

In 1910 I had the honour of being asked to address the Synod of the Episcopal Church of Ireland at its annual meeting in Dublin. As far as I know this was the first time for a Presbyterian minister to receive such an invitation. The reception given to me proved that there were no ecclesiastical swathes and bandages round the hearts of my Episcopal brethren preventing them from giving a most cordial welcome to a minister belonging to another communion than their own.

The present Primate of that Church, when Bishop of Down, presided at a great Catch-my-Pal demonstration in the Presbyterian Assembly Hall, Belfast. He said he was a teetotaller before I was born. At the beginning of my speech I told him that we welcomed him as a pal, but that I noticed he was an unadorned one, as he had not donned the button. I asked him if he would let me put the button in his coat, and he rose and received the button amid thundering applause from nearly three thousand pals. I said, "My Lord, it is said that I catch pals. I have caught a bishop to-night, and you will be as good a pal as any of us. And now I lay upon your lordship's shoulders the responsibility of going and catching every bishop on the bench." This statement was received with great enthusiasm, and the bishop promised to do what he could, and that one of the first things would be to go to the meeting of English bishops at Lambeth and to tell them all about the Catch-my-Pal movement. This he did, and with much effect, as I found when I went to London.

Great open-air demonstrations have been held all over the country. The first of these was at Banbridge on Easter Monday, 1910, attended by about 7,000 members. ˙ On that day the saloon-keepers organised steeplechases at the other side of the town, but the temperance demonstration was the more attractive meeting of the two, though one of the horses that won a race at the 'chases was called *Catch-my-Pal.*

The first Anniversary Demonstration was held at Armagh on 16th July, 1910, attended by about 5,000 members. On that day the Lord Primate, Dr. Alexander, aged 82, sent the following message: "My dear Friends, on a day so dear to you I send you an old man's message and benediction.. . . . . Unfortunately, for centuries, abstainers, total or even partial, were as uncommon as blackbirds among birds. But such a splendid exception do we find in the great Dr. Johnson. He calls himself 'a hardened and shameless tea-drinker.' He speaks of tea as 'this fascinating plant'; with tea he amuses the evening, with tea he solaces the midnight, and with tea he welcomes the morning. We are not able or required to do all this, but it marks out the greatest total abstainer of the seventeenth century.

"I dwell for a few moments on the consecrated unselfishness of the Catch-my-Pal which makes the convinced total abstainer first seek his brother or sister. . . . .

"I would pray for a blessing on the object of this gathering, and upon the originator of this movement whose success has been so widely recognised, and not without its effect in London, upon his helpers and upon all who are associated in this work. The Lord bless you all. . . ."

On that anniversary day it was considered a pious duty on the part of all good pals to pay a visit to the Manse, outside which was a placard in blue with the inscription:

HERE CATCH-MY-PAL WAS BORN, 16TH JULY, 1909,

and all day long crowds hung around the now famous lamp-post. Although the movement was just coming out of its swaddling clothes it had already got its relics and shrines, things that count immensely in any new faith.

About 10,000 marched through the streets of Belfast, a few days before the 16th, to a meeting in Ormeau Park, presided over by Alderman Mercier, J. P., first President of the Union, and a few days after it about 5,000 gathered at Baronscourt, where they were graciously welcomed by the Duke and Duchess of Abercorn. On that day the Duke's steward made cloakroom arrangements for 500 bicycles. The 500 tickets were used and 500 additional bicycles were stored without tickets! It was believed that this was the biggest display of bicycles ever seen in Ireland.

I have addressed many thousands of pals at excursions to our sea-side resorts, such as Portrush, Bundoran, Donaghadee, Newcastle, and Warrenpoint. My whole time during the Summers since the start of the Crusade has been occupied in addressing demonstrations of local or district dimensions. Nothing so helps to form public opinion as "the sound of the tread of marching feet," and, in these open-air demonstrations, many men and women are glad of the opportunity of showing what side they are on, in company with great numbers gathered together in a good cause.

Our second anniversary demonstration was held in Belfast on 10th June, 1911. It was difficult to calculate how many were present, but *The Northern Whig* stated in an editorial that it was probably the largest temperance procession seen in Ireland since the days of Father Mathew.

CHAPTER XVII

Catch-my-Pal in Scotland

THE Crusade could not be confined to Ireland. It is not like a Scotch road along which an Irish Presbyterian minister was motoring. He was not sure of his way, so he slowed down his motor and asked a little Scotch boy: "Where does this road go to?" And the laddie replied: "This road does na gae onywhaur; it just stays whaur it is."

For some weeks before Christmas, 1909, I had been receiving invitations to visit various places in Great Britain; and in the last week in December I addressed two meetings in Scotland, the first in Bellshill, and the second in Carrubbers' Close, Edinburgh. The good folk in Edinburgh were much astonished at the story I told them, and some seemed to "hae their doots about it." When I sat down, a gentleman rushed up from the body of the hall to the platform and began to speak. The chairman tried to stop him as the hour was late and he was not on the programme. But he would not be put down. He said: "I want to give my testimony. I have been travelling all over the North of Ireland and have seen how this movement is working; and I just want to say that Mr. Patterson might have said much more than he has said and still have been well within the bounds of truth." This quite unexpected and unsolicited testimony much gratified me. I have had an almost continual temptation to exaggerate when addressing public meetings, but I have ever tried to keep myself so "well within the bounds of truth" that no one could accuse me of over-stating my case.

On the first Sunday of 1910 I had a rousing experience in Glasgow, when I addressed a meeting in the Palace Theatre, there being about 1,500 men present. At the close of my address the whole audience seemed, in response to my appeal, to rise, to hold up their hands, to repeat the pledge, to clench their hands, and to say in crescendo style, "WE—WILL—SEE—THIS—THING—THROUGH." A gentleman said to me as we were coming out, "I never saw a Scotch audience rise like that before."

The next time I was in Scotland I addressed the Annual meeting of the British Women's Temperance Association in the Music Hall in Aberdeen. It was a wonderful sight. It was said there were about 2,000 persons present. I told my story, and practically every person present rose and repeated a total abstinence pledge and the Catch-my-Pal watchword. The following morning one of the leading temperance workers in Aberdeen told me that the age of miracles was not past yet. I asked him why he said so, and he said he never saw an Aberdeen audience get to their feet in such a mannar before, and that if *that* could be done in Aberdeen it could be done anywhere! This was delightful encouragement to me, for I had been told many a time that Scotland would not be caught as Ireland was. But, "if that could be done in Aberdeen!" then surely there was hope.

I have paid many visits to Scotland. Perhaps my greatest success was in Paisley, where I started a branch on a Sunday night in April, 1910, at a meeting in the Town Hall. Four hundred persons took the pledge, and since then about five thousand members have been enrolled. I do not know any town where the ministers threw themselves more heartily into this movement than in Paisley; and I believe it was their united and wholehearted action that contributed more than anything else to the splendid result achieved by the movement there. I started a branch in Inverness at the end of November, 1911. Before Christmas the Catch-my-Pal members united with the British Women's Total Abstinence branch in taking over a public-house and converting it into a Catch-my-Pal Café. Three hundred pledges were taken in that café in January, 1912, and the crusade began operations in two other districts in the town with such effect that *The Highland Times* said "Judging by the scarcity of drunks the Catch-my-Pal movement is doing really effective work. It has, in fact, worked a miracle which the most effective police court in the country has tried to perform and tried in vain."

One of my most interesting and pleasant Scotch experiences was my being invited to address a meeting of the Diocesan Temperance Society of Edinburgh, presided over by the bishop and attended by nearly all the Episcopal clergy of the city. They were much interested in my story, and seemed surprised at what I had to say about the approaches the Protestant churches of Ireland were making to one another. I said: "Well, you are Episcopalians and I am a Presbyterian and I am here among you to-night at any rate."

One Saturday I was advertised in the Edinburgh papers to give an address on the following afternoon in the Central Hall, Tollcross, on *"Catch-my-Pal; or How to be Happy though Sober."* *The Evening Dispatch* remarked: "We notice in our advertising columns that a certain gentleman is going to lecture in Edinburgh to-morrow on 'How to be Happy though Sober.' This will make us pause and consider what an admirable lecture some of us could give on *'How to be Miserable though Drunk.'* "

Eleven hundred men attended my meeting at Tollcross. I told them my story. They were much interested. The response to my appeal, however, was not as hearty as I expected, so I made another one, saying: "I was travelling recently in an Irish railway carriage and saw this conundrum written on the paint above the cushions: 'Why are the cushions in this carriage like Scotchmen?' I wonder if any of you can tell me the answer?" (I waited for a moment and no one replied.) "Well, it was evidently a Scotchman travelling in Ireland who wrote that conundrum there. Look at it again. Every word of it is important. 'Why—are—the—cushions—in—this—carriage—like—Scotchmen?' *'Because they never are beaten!'*" The eleven hundred men cheered, rolled the answer as a sweet morsel under their tongues, cheered again and settled down into a great calm of satisfaction. "But," I said, "the pity is that the answer is not true!" (Consternation!) "And, why do I say it is not true? Because of what I saw last New Year's Eve around the Tron Kirk. I had always thought of Scotland, the land of my forefathers, as the most Christian country in the world. Edinburgh is, I suppose, the most beautiful city in the world. There is not a better churched city in the world. For its size I believe no city in the world has better preachers. And yet, what did I see at the Tron Kirk on New Year's Eve? A veritable hell! On that night, above all others, when the heart of Scotland should have been looking up for guidance to live better in the coming year than it did in the one that was passing, it seemed as if, in a scene of drunken debauchery, Edinburgh was glorying in her shame. If a New Guinea savage could have viewed from an aeroplane the sight I saw he would likely have flown back to his savagery, saying: 'If Christianity can tolerate *that* in Edinburgh, then none of it for me. I prefer to be as I am.' Did it not seem as if the drink demon had Scotland by the very throat that night? Your Lord Rosebery says that if the State does not throttle the drink-traffic the drink-traffic will throttle the State. May I not shelter myself behind Lord Rosebery when I say that, judging by the Tron Kirk scene, the drink was throttling Scotland? At any rate, as long as such a scene is tolerated by Scotch public opinion, it cannot be said that 'Scotchmen never are beaten.' *They are beaten, beaten by the drink!* And I ask all here who wish to help in forming such a public opinion in Scotland as to make these Hogmanay debaucheries an impossibility in your land, I ask all of you, sons of 'Scots wha hae wi' Wallace bled,' who would like to see the drink curse driven from your country, to rise to your feet and shut your fists and say: 'We will see this thing through!'" I think every man in the hall rose to his feet. And when eleven hundred voices said word by word, "We will see this thing through," one felt as if Hogmanay as now witnessed would soon be as only an unpleasant memory in the land.

I know that Scotland appears at her worst at New Year's time. But that is the time she should appear at her best. I suppose there are no better Christian or temperance workers anywhere in the world than in Scotland, and all readers of this book will unite with me in hoping that Scotland, when she puts her Local Option Act into operation in 1920, will do such exploits under it as to set the pace for the rest of the United Kingdom in the race for sobriety and purity of life.

In some places in Scotland friends did not care to venture on the formation of a new temperance society where so many societies already existed. They said: "We'll hear what you have got to say and we'll hold a committee." In not a few instances the committee sat, and so sat on Catch-my-Pal that Catch-my-Pal never rose again! But I am grateful to be able to say that wherever the movement got a chance in Scotland it did as good work as it did in Ireland.

CHAPTER XVIII

CATCH-MY-PAL IN ENGLAND

In April, 1910, I went to address my first meeting in England. It was the annual meeting of the Women's Total Abstinence Union, held in Caxton Hall, Westminster. Delegates from all parts of England were present and honoured me with a most sympathetic hearing. One of the results of my address was that Catch-my-Pal enthusiasm fired to finer service many of the best workers among the women of England. The Catch-my-Pal aggressive method was introduced into many branches of the Women's Total Abstinence Union throughout the country, and from that Union and from the British Women's Temperance Association I have received, and am still receiving, invitations to conduct meetings from Southampton to Northumberland.

While in London I addressed other meetings at Putney, where I started the first Catch-my-Pal branch in England, and at Norwood, where I had a singular experience. The meeting was in St. Andrew's Church. When the chairman and I came out of the vestry to the pulpit the great audience rose to their feet. I wondered what this meant. The organist began to play the Dead March in Saul! King Edward VII. had died two days before. At the close of the March I had to rise to try to enthuse for total abstinence an audience clad in mourning for our King!

I am always nervous when about to address an audience, but never did I feel so much inclined to go and hide myself as I did before I got up to speak in the

73

City Temple pulpit at the annual meeting of the Congregational Union of England and Wales. I remembered that at a great united meeting in London a Presbyterian minister rose to speak immediately before Dr. Parker. He was duly impressed by his position, and said: "I'll be brief and make way for Dr. Parker, as I am but a humble Presbyterian minister." When Dr. Parker got to his feet he said, in his great rotund style: "When I heard the previous speaker say, 'I am but a humble Presbyterian minister,' I said to myself, 'I will now turn aside and see this GREAT SIGHT!'" If I never felt it before, I felt on that night that I was "but a humble Presbyterian minister." I saw the shade of Parker turning aside to see me in his pulpit. I felt as if I must shrivel up into nothingness under his gaze and, for the first few moments on my feet, I thought the audience saw my hair all standing on end.

There were other reasons besides for my nervousness that night. I had one of the greatest surprises of my life, when, one morning in Armagh, early in 1910, I received a letter from Mr. J. Turner Rae, Secretary of the National Temperance League, asking me, in the name of his committee, to conduct a campaign in London in the October of that year. For some time I could not entertain the idea, and was on the point of declining the invitation had not my wife said to me: "Of course you'll go to London. No other man has a story like yours, and 'if it has done so much good here, why should you not go and tell it in London?" So I wrote to Mr. Rae, accepting the invitation. I knew *he* was in the City Temple audience, and I felt that my address in the Temple was my testimonial for the London campaign. It was not till the following morning, when I received a card from Mr. Rae, that I was at ease and began to look forward to October in hope.

As I consider my London campaign the most important one I have yet attempted, I shall be forgiven if I give here an extract from Mr. Rae's report of it in *The National Temperance Quarterly*, December, 1910.

"A LONDON AWAKENING."

"One of the most remarkable temperance efforts of modern times was carried out in the Metropolis during the month of October, under the auspices of the National Temperance League. The London papers had for some time been giving most interesting accounts of the marvellous success attending the efforts of the Rev. Robert J. Patterson, LL.B., of Armagh, in redeeming the North of Ireland from the social conditions set up by the drinking habits of the people. Commencing in an exceedingly small way 'round a lamp-post' in the city of Armagh, in July, 1909, the Catch-my-Pal movement had resulted in little more than fifteen months in the accession of some 140,000 persons to the total abstinence pledge.

"For some considerable time the committee of the League had been anxious to discover a means by which the practice of abstinence from alcohol could be made to appeal more convincingly to the numerous social agencies for men which have sprung up within recent years. The committee realise that this is absolutely essential to the success of other movements kindred to their own, and are convinced that until this is appreciated by leaders and members their ultimate aims cannot be reached.

"Accordingly, the Committee took advantage of the opportunity afforded by Mr. Patterson's New Crusade to endeavour to awaken the interest of London social reformers, and incidentally to arouse inactive abstainers and members of temperance societies to renewed effort in the enrolment of individuals as workers in the Total Abstinence Cause. This aim has been fully fulfilled, as some six thousand three hundred pledges have already been secured.

"The possibilities of the continued work of such an army as this are so great as to be impossible of conception, and it only requires a corresponding financial coöperation to that of the personal work to create such a change in the Metropolis as will produce similar results in relation to industry and commerce as have been produced in the North of Ireland, where, according to a *Daily Telegraph* correspondent, 'men are now paying their debts, children are being better fed and clothed, and a higher standard of living prevails among the people. The butcher, baker, grocer, shoemaker and draper are all benefitting by the spending with them of the large sums of money formerly wasted in drink. In the City of Londonderry last winter more children's boots were sold than ever before in the same period. The life of the policeman has become, in reality, a happy one, and cases are few and far between in towns where they were formerly numerous.'

"The question has been asked whether the pledges are wholly 'new,' and the estimate shows that about one-third (two-sixths) are old abstainers who have been inspired to work; about one-sixth are active workers who feel that the Catch-my-Pal method is a valuable adjunct to their methods; and about one-half (three-sixths) are those of new recruits to abstinence. The spiritual, moral, and material effects of such a body of workers cannot fail to be seen in the amelioration of the poverty, crime, and disease which are the direct result of the drinking customs. The Committee of the League rejoice at the undoubted stimulus which the visit of the Rev. Robert J. Patterson has given to the temperance work in the Metropolis, as evidenced by the further operations in every branch of the Christian Church, among the Men's Societies of various kinds and all temperance organisations.

"With an aggregate attendance of some 24,000

persons, the thirty meetings which comprised the calendar of London engagements were supported by the leaders of every branch of religious, social, and temperance work in the different localities in which the gatherings took place, and, moreover, were characterised by the display of such a note of enthusiasm as must have called to mind the scenes of 'those earlier times' to many a veteran who happened to be present.

"The seven special afternoon gatherings, appealing more particularly to women, were of a most encouraging nature. The evening demonstrations took place in nineteen of the more important town and public halls, and these, with few exceptions, were crowded to their utmost capacity, over 3,000 people occupying the Peckham Hippodrome, and 2,500 the Conference Hall at Stratford. Two other particularly noteworthy gatherings were those which took place in the Wandsworth Town Hall, at which, notwithstanding the facilities for an overflow meeting, many had to be turned away from the doors; and at Greenwich Royal Hospital Schools, where Mr. Patterson had the opportunity of addressing the 1,000 sailor boys forming the League's Naval Band of Hope. Here many remarkable scenes have taken place, but, in the words of an eye-witness, 'never could there have been a more inspiring occasion.' Firmly gripping the attention of the boys, Mr. Patterson pressed home his most telling appeal on behalf of total abstinence, until with their enthusiasm at white heat the boys rose in one great body and voiced, in such a way as only young British tars know how to vociferate, their intention to 'see this thing through,' cheer upon cheer following their adoption of the following pledge: 'For God and Home and Native Land, I hereby promise, with God's help, to abstain from all alcoholic beverages, and to get as many others as I can to do the same.'

"A farewell public rally took place in the Holborn Hall, when, under the chairmanship of the League's venerable President, a large and enthusiastic gathering of workers demonstrated their appreciation of Mr. Patterson's coming into their midst. A most interesting reception preceded the 'Farewell' public meeting. This was attended by a large number of the clergy and ministers of all denominations, as well as by a most representative company of temperance friends who, though they sympathised with Mr. Patterson when he confessed that, notwithstanding the results of the crusade, he found more encouragement among hard headed Aberdonians than in London, yet heartily agreed that a truly marvellous work had been done. In their fitting testimonies, however, as President and Chairman, respectively, of the League, the Dean of Hereford and Mr. Robert Whyte, jun., warmly concurred with the view expressed by Mr. Rae, that their having taken some six thousand pledges was exceedingly encouraging, in that it must undoubtedly result in the permeation of the temperance factor amongst all the other great social movements which the League has endeavoured to reach, and finally, in such an awakening throughout the country as will bring nearer and nearer the true realisation of the fact finely expressed by Mr. Whyte in the words:

"It's not by Eastern windows only,
　When daylight comes, comes in the light;
In front the sun climbs slow, how slowly,
　But Westward look, the land is bright."

"We cannot do better than conclude with the following fine impression of one of the Crusade meetings, contributed by the Rev. Gerald Thomson, M.A., Secretary of the Church of England Temperance Society, to the *Temperance Chronicle*, which gives an excellent idea of the character and method of Mr. Patterson's appeal: 'It is not everyone, perhaps, who is familiar with the Lambeth Baths. Personally I know them well—in their winter guise and employment of an Assembly Hall. It was, therefore, no very new experience for me to find myself one of the crowd of Pals, and would-be Pals, who came on Wednesday of last week to hear the Rev. R. J. Patterson, Catch-my-Pal leader—the originator (humanly speaking) of the movement. I say 'humanly speaking,' for it is quite clear that this is a God-sent wave, and that the eloquent Irishman, whose name is known wherever the English language and Temperance are associated, is the instrument—neither more nor less. And no man would be so ready to acknowledge this as R. J. Patterson himself. This brings me to the man himself. We in England do not know the Presbyterian Minister intimately, and I confess that I looked upon the first and best Pal of the Society—now numbering 140,000—with much interest. There is nothing of the impossible comic paper 'Pastor' about Patterson. Neatly dressed in correct clerical attire, clean shaven, and with a slight natural 'tonsure,' he would pass for a priest of our own Church or, in view of the thin patch at the back of his head, of the Italian Mission in this country. I had not been two minutes in the presence of the man before I knew why he had been chosen for the great work. Then there is the charm of manner and utter absence of affectation that would, and do, commend him to every man, woman, and child with whom he comes into contact—the personal magnetism that is a necessary part of the equipment of an Apostle. Lastly, there is the extraordinary eloquence of the man. Oh, that torrential eloquence! Never have I listened to anything like it. In a ringing voice, with never a falter, we at Lambeth were swept along for an hour and a half. At one moment we were in fits of laughter as the Irishman told with all his native drollery of some decisive victory over the 'Dhrink.' The next minute we caught our breaths and leaned forward as the minister warned us in solemn tones of our own terrible responsibility. We were distressed spectators of the miserable, drink-sodden home; we cowered with the starving children as the drunken father cursed them and their mother in the filthy hovel occupied by the drunkard's family. We cheered with the second batch of thirty-one newly enrolled pals, who crowded 'his rivrence's' dining-room in Armagh a fortnight after the game of catching pals had started. We bowed our heads with the newly enrolled brotherhood as the minister thanked Almighty God for His mercies. We rode on a jaunting car to Portadown with his 'rivrence,' and there we met another car manned by six men who had been 'the biggest dhrunkards in the city,' and who now are its most fanatical abstainers. We said that we would 'see this thing through.' Suddenly we were at the Battle of Trafalgar, sent there by a thousand twentieth century Greenwich boys to find out whether the rank and file did really win that great fight. And then, as we of the 95th Regiment grasped our long muskets at Waterloo, and wondered whether we could hold out, Wellington came and cheered us on by telling us that we had *got* to win, and from then each man fought his own musket all he knew till the day was ours. And suddenly we were back in Armagh standing in a small circle of light cast by a street lamp, and hearing a typical Irishman telling 'his rivrence' that the very few drinkers left in the primatial city were afraid to come near that lamp-post —by which the first six pals were caught—lest they 'should take the infecshion.' And—I write it with all reverence—in spite of the humour and the laughter, in spite of the occasional gentle digs, in spite of everything, we felt all through that we were not far from the Great Founder of our Faith, that it is His work, and that its marvellous success—second only to that of Father Mathew's incredible campaign—is due to the fact that the work is carried on in His name. No politics is the rule—and, better still, is a rule that is kept. No denominationalism is another rule—the whole thing was grand and inspiring, and, above all, spiritual. That is the secret of Robert J, Patterson's success—he is in deadly earnest, and he is truly spiritual. God bless and prosper him!"

I have addressed meetings in about fifty English towns from Plymouth to York, and from Weston-super-Mare to Dover. The enthusiasm at these meetings has been as great as at any meetings in Ireland. In many places the temperance friends did not see their way to start a new society, but adopted the Catch-my-Pal idea in connection with existing societies. In other places branches of Catch-my-Pal have been started with splendid results. In one town many great drinkers were enrolled in a very short time. The enthusiastic secretary, who is an Irishman, had his men formed into companies, with a captain over each company. These companies are sent out weekly for recruiting purposes, and much friendly competition is fostered among them in catching pals. The names of the companies are "The Stick-at-ems," "The Pick-em-ups," "The Pal-catchers," "The Scouts.", The secretary writes to say that all these companies work hand in hand for the reclaiming of the drunkard.

A good Irish doctor started a branch in his town in Cheshire. He brought me to see an artisan's wife whom he called a "wonderful woman." When I entered her little kitchen I saw a really wonderful face, a face beaming with goodness and happiness. The doctor asked her to show me her book. She handed me a small note-book. I turned over page after page and saw nothing but names. I asked what all these names meant, and my friend said: "These are names of persons this good woman has brought into our Catch-my-Pal Society."

How many had she brought in? Five? Yes. Twelve? Yes. Twenty-seven? Yes. Forty-three? Yes. Seventy-six? Yes. Eighty-nine? Yes. Ninety-eight? Yes. One hundred and five? Yes. She brought in *one hundred and five!* Perhaps some good English, Scotch or Irish woman who reads this will say: "Well, if she had paid proper attention to her house perhaps she would not have had so much time to pay attention to other people." But I never saw a sweeter little kitchen. It was twinkling and winking at me from the knob on the door to the knob on the range. Everything was in its place. There was every indication that the good woman did pay attention to her own home and was doing all that in her lay to promote the cause of total abstinence by getting others to join the Union and learn to make their homes happy too.

At one of my meetings in England a lady came to the front and asked me did I want her to sign the pledge. I said I did. She pointed to a little white bow on her bosom and said: "But I am a member of The British Women's Temperance Association." When she was asked *how many persons she had been the means of bringing into the membership of her branch of that Society during the year* she had to confess with some hesitancy that she had not brought in a single member. She was then asked to sign the pledge and become a *worker*.

Perhaps the most interesting meeting I had the pleasure of addressing in England was one in Plymouth workhouse. I was attending the annual meetings of the Western Temperance League, and was asked to go to speak to the people in the workhouse. The next day the following report was in a local paper: "There was a remarkable scene in the dining hall in Plymouth workhouse last evening . . . Mr. Patterson alternately gently chided the women and soundly castigated those of the men who owed their position to drink, and finally got his entire audience to stand, as expressing their desire to see their land freed from drink. Then, with very few exceptions, men and women alike, young and old, feeble and strong, raised

82

their right hands and took the Catch-my-Pal pledge, vowing earnestly that they would 'see this thing through.' It was a wonderful tableau."

In January, 1912, I had a mission in Jersey, Guernsey, and the Isle of Wight. It was computed that in twelve nights I addressed over eleven thousand people and that the meeting held in Guernsey under the presidency of the Lieutenant-Governor was the largest one ever held in the island, there being about 2,500 persons present. Many pledges were taken, and from reports I have received from all parts of England and from the Islands, Good Samaritanship is busy along Catch-my-Pal lines in lifting up the fallen and bringing in the outcast.

CHAPTER XIX

CATCH-MY-PAL IN WALES

I was invited to address three meetings in Cardiff in October, 1910, and the North Wales Temperance Federation invited me to conduct a campaign within its area in April, 1911. The Rev. J. Glyn Davies, of Rhyl, arranged my meetings. In a published report of this campaign Mr. Davies said, *inter alia:*

"The Rev. R. J. Patterson has just concluded a week's work in North Wales, visiting Llandudno, Bangor, Denbigh, Rhyl, Mold, Wrexham, Machynlleth, Aberystwyth, and Connah's Quay. And a rare week it has been. While the temperance sentiment is clear and strong in North Wales, perhaps clearer and stronger than in any other part of the United Kingdom, yet owing to difficulties of language and religion and politics, united temperance action is almost impossible. Not only is sect supreme, but the bilingual hindrance is most grievously real. Mr. Patterson's meetings brought the sects and the tongues together in a wonderful manner. . . . We knew that he had started a great movement, and that it had spread, man bringing man, and pal catching pal, till Ireland had become a messenger of hope to the rest of the Kingdom. When he came he was not a stranger. We prepared our best centres for him, took the biggest buildings, printed the bravest placards, made a highway of hope for his coming. Crowds gathered to his hearing. Englishmen and Welshmen, churchmen and chapelmen, abstainers and drinkers, they have gathered in their hundreds, and it has been wonderful in our sight. It was not a League football match, nor yet a Lloyd George meeting; it was just simply a temperance gathering. The buildings were full; the spirit was grand; the success was complete. In collegiate towns like Bangor and Aberystwyth, in seaside resorts like Rhyl and Llandudno, in busy centres like Mold and Wrexham and Connah's Quay, in inland towns like Denbigh and Machynlleth, all along the line, everywhere alike, the crusade caught on. . . .

"No man can do much who does not know and who does not feel that he has been called and sent. *Mr. Patterson has this unmistakable power, he knows that God has called him. What an inspiration it is! How it sustains him! How it fires him! How it puts into him the patience, the perseverance, the pluck of a man who has a work to do, and cannot yield, cannot rest, cannot die till that work is done. The deliverance of the drunkard—there is his one work. To that he is called; thereto he is bound. He is a man of one work.* . . . I should not call him an orator. God save us from orators! . . . the vehemence of it all, body, blood, brain, in passion and storm, it all but swept us off our feet. We cheered and laughed and cried. We signed the pledge; we shook our fists; *we went out to fight the drink as we have never fought it yet. What else could we do?*

"As he himself says, he has got a 'story to tell.' That is all. He is not a temperance lecturer; he does not presume to be an expert on the temperance question. He knows little of the 'action of alcohol on the heart and the stomach and the kidneys,' as he himself told us. I never heard him mention *delirium tremens* and cirrhosis of the liver. I doubt whether he has ever read Horsley and Sturge. But—and oh! what a BUT —he has a 'story to tell.' And such a story! A wonderful story! One of the stories of a century! . . . Some cynics will doubtless decry his methods; but when these will have a 'story to tell,' a great story of

85

some noble work started by themselves, they can well dare to criticise. Till then they had better hold their tongues.

"He has given us a new idea, simple, but noble, 'Catch-my-Pal.' Why did we not think of it before? He has roused us, united us, started us on a new fresh quest. *He has given temperance work a new turn and temperance workers a new spirit.* Surely that is a precious service."

One of the outstanding features of the meetings in Wales was the attendance of so many ministers on the platform. With a few exceptions of places in Ireland and England, nowhere have I received such enthusiastic encouragement from ministers as in Wales.

Many pledges to work more earnestly in the temperance cause were taken in the course of the campaign. Branches were formed not only in places I visited but in other places through correspondence. The results of the few meetings addressed by me in the Principality are embodied in the following resolution I had the honour of receiving from the Federation some weeks after the close of the campaign:

"That we place on record our very deep gratitude to the Rev. R. J. Patterson for his visit to North Wales, for his splendid advocacy of the principles of temperance, especially as they bear upon the duty and responsibility of the individual, for the very real impetus he has given to temperance among us, and for the hope we have that the seed he has sown will next winter bear abundant fruit in renewed energy and zeal."

CHAPTER XX

CATCH-MY-PAL BECOMING WORLD-WIDE

I HAD the great honour of an invitation to address the International Congress on Alcoholism at The Hague in September, 1911. I felt about it as I did about the invitation to London. But when I thought of all God' had wrought through the simple story I had to tell, I believed He would use it on the Continent as in the United Kingdom. I addressed the Congress on three occasions. On one of them I told my story. The effect of my address is best described in the words of a German priest who, when I came down from the platform, came and shook hands with me and said, as he pointed to his head and his heart: "I thank you for what you have said; it has not only appealed to my head, it has also touched my heart." I did not understand many of the speeches, delivered as they were in foreign tongues; but I gathered from the printed synopses of them that very few of them dealt with the Temperance Problem from the point of view of individual responsibility. The Catch-my-Pal story deals with the problem along personal lines which will eventually lead into legislative action. I may be wrong, but *I think too many reformers are trying to work along legislative lines while neglecting the personal endeavour which forms the public opinion on which legislative action depends.*

Many friends, unknown to me, have written me to say that Catch-my-Palism is "just the thing we want." Many of the members of The Hague Congress, from many countries, expressed themselves to me in the same way. Good Samaritanship must always appeal to the head and touch the heart, and, while the Temperance Problem requires all the head we can give to it, it must get far more heart than it has ever yet got before those who want to solve it have proved themselves in deadly earnest in the face of a cynical world.

It was arranged that I should address the annual meeting of the Dutch "National Christian Teetotallers' Association" at Haarlem, at eleven o'clock on the morning of my arrival in Holland. I had received no instructions about hospitality, and when my wife and I arrived at ten o'clock there was no one to meet us at the station. I did not know where the meeting was to be held. No one at the station knew anything about it, but a porter who could speak a little English told me that a gentleman had been at the station expecting me by an earlier train. I surmised that this gentleman was to be my host, and that if I could find him I could find the place of meeting. I got his name on a piece of paper, Monsieur B——, Overveen. It was given to the driver of a four-wheeler. He drove to Overveen, almost two miles away. My speech was to be made at eleven o'clock, and it was now ten-thirty! I thought the driver would never stop. He could not understand me, and much less could I understand him. He drove on. His carriage was going, going, and so was the time! He arrived at a house, made enquiries, found he was on the wrong trail, went to another house, rang the bell, told his story, and seemed to stand in blank wonderment before the maid. I essayed an enquiry, but could convey no idea. No Monsieur B. lived there in any case. Several servants, both outdoor and indoor, gathered around us and our four-wheeler. They chattered, and my wife and I chattered. I saw a young gentleman passing through the grounds and hailed him with: "Do you speak English?"

"Yah, yah, a leetle."

"Can you tell me where Monsieur B. lives?"

"Nah, nah."

"Can you tell me where the Post Office is?"

He did not understand. Stuck again!

"Can you tell me where the telegraph is?"

"Yah, yah, telegraaf and post, telegraaf and post, yah, yah."

I asked him to direct my driver to the telegraaf. He did so.

"Do you think he knows where he is to go?" I asked.

"Yah, yah."

"Well, tell him again," I said.

He told him again, and off we drove. When we arrived at the Telegraph Office I ran in and said: "Does anyone here speak English?"

A young Dutchman came forward and said: "Yes, I speak English."

"Can you tell me where Monsieur B. lives here?"

"Oh, yes, he lives quite near this."

I asked that my driver should be directed, so he came out and directed him.

"Do you think he knows where to go?" I asked.

"Oh, yes."

"Well, tell him again, if you please."

He told him again, and we drove off again, accompanied by a telegraph boy on a bicycle, sent by the young Dutchman to make sure we arrived.

We drove up a fine avenue through stately trees to a lordly mansion. Monsieur B. lived there, but he was not at home. Neither was Madame B.; and the maid could not tell my driver where they had gone! Stuck again! It was now eleven o'clock, and I was booked for a speech at eleven at a meeting of the National Christian Teetotallers' Association!

Bewilderment was settling down upon my wife and myself and the four-wheeler and the horse and the whip, when, all of a sudden, the equally bewildered maid rushed into the house and left my wife and myself and the horse and the whip all staring at one another in that four-wheeler! Very soon there was a rush out of the house.

A young lady came bounding over to me and greeted me: "Are you Mr. Patterson?" She was English!

"You are one of God's good angels to me this day among all these barbarians!" I jokingly replied.

She explained everything, told me that our host and hostess were at the meeting, where the meeting was, how much I should pay the driver, and so on. I asked her to tell the driver where to go. She did so. I asked her if she thought he understood where to go.

"Oh, yes."

"Well, please tell him again."

She told him again, and we trotted off and arrived just as the meeting was ready for me, as my predecessor on the platform had exceeded his time.

I gave my address through Miss Crommelin, treasurer of The Hague Congress, who kindly acted as interpreter, and I received much applause when I told the audience that it was the first meeting I had addressed outside my own country. My story evidently entered the hearts of many there, and I found that what went home in Ireland and Great Britain was not lost in Holland. But I found also that the delay of interpreting was a great hindrance to enthusiasm. I was much delighted to find that information about the movement had been given in several Dutch papers and magazines, and that most of those whom I addressed were already familiar with my story.

Two days after the meeting in Haarlem I went to Arnhem to address a popular meeting which had been arranged by telegram from Belfast on the previous Saturday. The lady who wired me had worked up a splendid audience, which I addressed through a Dutch minister as interpreter. Sixty-three persons signed the

Catch-my-Pal pledge and "took the button" and did their recruiting work with most encouraging success. As I now write I have received a letter to say that there are four hundred pals in the Arnhem branch.

This letter tells me that the Catch-my-Pal movement is now being organised in connection with the National Christian Teetotallers' Association, as the temperance workers do not think it wise to have a separate society. The National Association has appointed a special Catch-my-Pal Committee to further the aggressive movement all over the country. It is interesting to read that "the Roman Catholics have copied the Catch-my-Pal pledge card. The more pals are caught the better, but we think it wiser that each denomination should catch for its own society." "We would have asked you to come back to Holland again to address meetings, but we were afraid you would found a separate society with a too strongly marked Irish stamp. Now, I think, when our organisation is a little more complete, this fear will be greatly lessened; you will then come to an existing organisation."

The Dutch have two ways of saying "Catch-my-Pal," namely: "Vang mijn Kameraad," and "Pak mijn Maat." As I was going to my host's house one day at Haarlem I was not sure of my way. I met a young gentleman of whom I enquired the way. He said he would walk with me. He seemed curious about me, a foreigner, and asked where I came from. I told him I was an Irishman. He was immediately turned into a bundle of notes of interrogation. No man stirs up so much curiosity in the bosom of a foreigner as an Irishman. He seems to be *an international puzzle.* My friend asked me what I was doing in Holland, and I told him I had come over to address the Congress on alcoholism at The Hague. He had read about the Congress. Then he asked me what I had spoken about. I said I had come to speak about the "Vang mjin Kameraad" movement. He shook his head in very solemn fashion, with a blank look in his eyes, and said "Nah, nah."

I ventured on the other name, and said I had been speaking on the "Pak mijn Maat" movement. The same blank look came into his eyes. Evidently he knew nothing of "paking maats." Then I thought I would venture on plain English, so I said I had been speaking on the "Catch-my-Pal" movement. He almost whirled me into the hedge in the vehemence of his gesticulation as he showed his recognition of the name, and said:

"Oh, yah, yah, yah, yah, Catch-ma-Pal, Catch-ma-Pal, Catch-ma-Pal, oh, yah, yah, yah, yah." It was very gratifying to find a Dutchman by the wayside in his own country who seemed familiar with the name that some of my own countrymen despised. And it is also very gratifying that this little book, which was published first in London in August, 1912, was translated into Dutch by the Rev. I. van Dorp, D.D., of Gendringen, Holland, and published in that language, early in 1913.

I had never been on the Continent before. While I was charmed with the flowers of Holland, admired its towns, enjoyed its splendid hospitality, and was amazed at its "Lesson in Anatomy," I was disappointed in the country. An Irishman was travelling through the Highlands of Scotland. He remarked to a fellow travelling in the train "That wud be a very livil counthry, yir honour, only fur thim hills." And I thought, as I went about in the Dutch trains, that Holland would be a very hilly country only for "thim" plains. May she get her back up as a great mountain ridge in her determination to throw off the drink-yoke that is crushing so many of her people as flat as her fields!

A German professor who heard the Catch-my-Pal story at The Hague, went back to his home at Heidelberg and started a Catch-my-Pal branch. Some days afterwards I had the pleasure of receiving a letter from him, conveying to me the greetings of the first pals in Germany, and an assurance of his desire and determination to have the movement set a-going in the Fatherland.

Temperance enthusiasts and authorities in France, Switzerland and Denmark, have written on the movement in various magazines in their respective countries, and I have received from a friend in Denmark an assurance that he will do all in his power to have the movement, on which he has written several articles, introduced to his people, and this book translated into the Danish language.

An Irish chaplain started the work among the troops to whom he ministered on the coast of China, and a little history of the movement has been written in the Chinese language and published in China.

The movement is at work in nearly every British Colony, among the coloured people in Kingston, Jamaica and in Ibobo, West Africa, where there is a prosperous branch, and some time ago I had a request for information from a missionary in British East Africa who wanted to start the crusade among the pagan people there who are being ruined by rum.

AMERICA

SOME months after the movement started I was asked by many ministers and others when I intended to go to America. I said that I would not go till I was asked. They said that I should go as soon as possible, as the American papers had told all about the movement and the Americans would want to hear about it before it became a thing of yesterday. Certainly I did wish to go to America, but I did not care to push myself. I believed an invitation would come to me in God's good time, just as He, in His good time, enabled me to start the movement.

THE HAPPY ART OF CATCHING MEN

In 1912 the Rev. H. C. Minton, D.D., of Trenton, New Jersey, Ex-Moderator of the Presbyterian Church, and President of the National Reform Association of Pittsburgh, was in Ireland looking for material for the platform of The Second World's Christian Citizen Conference, to be held in Portland, Oregon, in July, 1913. He was in Belfast, June, 1912, at the annual meeting of the General Assembly of the Presbyterian Church in Ireland. I addressed the Assembly on the Temperance question, but I did not know he was there. Some time afterwards I had the honour of being invited by him to be the Irish speaker at that great Conference. I accepted the invitation and came to America in May, 1913.

Meetings were arranged for me by the Association on my way to and from Portland. I travelled twenty-one thousand miles in the United States in a little more than four months, and addressed many Chautauquas, Summer Assemblies, Ministerial Associations, Young Men's Associations, Church Synods, and Women's Christian Temperance Union Conferences and Rescue Missions.

Everywhere I went my message was received with much keenness and interest. Nearly everywhere I was told, "this is just the thing we want in temperance work." I did not organise the movement, as the time of the year and the personnel of the meetings were not favourable for organisation. I was out on an advertising tour, and I am glad to say that, as far as I can learn, my advertising was not in vain.

At least sixty thousand people repeated the Catch-my-Pal pledge at the meetings I addressed in America in 1913.

At the Portland Conference I addressed twelve thousand people on a Wednesday night, and fifteen thousand at the concluding meeting on the following Sunday. On both occasions the whole audience rose at my request and repeated the pledge and then closed

their fists and said, "We will see this thing through!"
I never saw such inspiring sights. It was worth my
while to travel all the way from Ireland to see them.
And yet there was a little Portland incident which com-
forted me more than all the enthusiasm in the great
meetings. One day I went into a great department
store. The manager of one of the departments accosted me and said, "Good evening, Mr. Patterson."
I said, "How do you know me?" And he answered,
"I was at the meeting on Wednesday night and heard
you speak. I had been a moderate drinker, but I never
drank to be drunk. My wife often asked me to give
up the drink altogether, but I never could see my way
to do so. Your appeal on Wednesday went home to
me in such a way that I could resist no longer. So,
when you asked us all to stand up and repeat the
pledge, I stood up and looked at my wife, and she
looked at me. With uplifted hand I repeated your
pledge and your watchword. Now the drink is gone
for ever from my life and my wife is as happy as
the day is long, and *I want to thank you for what you
have done for me.*"

I conducted a week's meeting in Detroit. As I
passed a church one day I saw that the Women's
Christian Temperance Union of Michigan was holding
its annual conference. I said to myself, "I'll go in and
hear what these women are talking about." I went
into the church and stood in a corner near the door.
A lady rose up and came towards the door. Just as
she was about to pass me she stopped and said to me,
"Can you tell me where the Rev. Mr. Patterson,
Catch-my-Pal, is to speak in Detroit to-morrow night?
I want to go to hear him." I said, "Well, this is funny
that you ask me this question?" And she asked me,
"Why is it funny?" "Well, you see, I am just the person you are enquiring about!" "And are you Mr. Pat-
terson?" On her being assured that it was even as
I had said she asked, "Does our president know you

are here?" I said that no one knew I was there, that I knew nobody there, and that I did not wish anyone to know I was there, as I was anxious to hear what the women had to say on the Temperance question. She immediately turned and said, "But our president must be told you are here." And away she walked up to the platform. The president came down to me and insisted on my going up to give an address. I said, "What about your printed programme?" She said, "O, never mind the printed programme. We must hear about Catch-my-Pal, and you can talk to us for half an hour." I 'talked' for half an hour, at the end of which about five hundred women rose to their feet, lifted their hands, repeated the pledge, shut their fists and said in the most vigorous manner, "We Will See This Thing Through!"

I have attended many meetings of women in America, and I have been delighted with the spirit of devoted determination they are showing in the fight against the drink. I have never heard better speaking than at some of these women's meetings. The leaders have a thorough grip of the subject and can express themselves in such clear and convincing language as to draw out the highest admiration of any mere man. It is a matter for great thankfulness that, through quiet and peaceable determination, the women of America are obtaining the franchise. The sooner all the women in the United States have obtained it the better it will be for the country, for I am sure *they will utilise it for upsetting the licensed trade* with an alacrity the men are not quick to show in dealing with social problems.

At one of the Women's Conferences I had an unusual experience. During the singing of the opening hymn the wind seemed to fail in the bellows of the organ, and it was in much desperation the organist played us through. I was not on my feet more than five minutes when the electric lights went out, and there we were all in the dark of an October night. I said, "The devil knows we are out against him to-night and he is at his old wily tricks. He punctured the organ bellows, and now he has side-tracked the electric current in the wires. He loves the darkness rather than the light because his deeds are evil. But I am an Irishman, and I am not going to let the devil get the better of me to-night. If you can hear in the dark I can talk in the dark and we will let the devil see that he is not our master yet." I talked away in the dark. It was very weird. I talked to an invisible audience for an hour and a half, and although I went away quite exhausted I felt that his Satanic majesty was worsted even in the dark!

One Sunday afternoon I addressed a great meeting of young men. The weather was so warm that nearly every man in the meeting took off his coat. I never addressed such a coatless crowd before. I was not long on my feet till I was apparently so hot that several men shouted to me, "Take off your coat!" I told them I had already taken off my coat in a more real way, perhaps, than some of them, as I had resigned my church and left my home that I might devote my life to a war against drink. I said it was an easy thing to take off the tailored stuff called a coat, for the purpose of making oneself comfortable on a warm day, but that *something more than that kind of coat-doffing was necessary in these days* when the battle was hot against the legalised curses of our country. At the end of my address I asked all the men who wished to take off their coats to fight against the drink to stand up. About 400 men rose to their feet with much enthusiasm and repeated the pledge and slogan to see the thing through.

It is gladdening to hear that the Railway Companies are ceasing to employ men who take drink. No man who likes drink can be depended upon to do the right thing in a sudden railway emergency. I understand that the Banking Companies are also clearing out the drinkers, as no drinker can be thoroughly relied upon in dealing quickly with serious financial transactions. If no drunkard shall inherit the kingdom of heaven, it is also being found that *no drunkard shall inherit the kingdom of earth.* In all my travelling over the United States I find, in conversation with all classes of people, that there is a rising tide of feeling after a way of clearing from before the feet of progress the drink hindrance which has blocked the way so long.

This feeling after a way has found articulate expression in the resolutions of the wonderful Conference held at Columbus, Ohio, in November, 1913, when it was unanimously decided to petition Congress to make a national prohibition amendment to the Constitution, and to work for national prohibition and *a Saloonless Nation in 1920.* At all my meetings I have brought this matter before the people, and it has been received with the greatest enthusiasm. *It seems to me that the United States are on the verge of taking the most momentous step on the way to National Purity and Progress ever taken by any nation. If this step is really taken, I have no doubt but that the United States will become the envy of every other nation under heaven.*

Many ministers at conferences and other meetings throughout the country have told me that they will adopt the Catch-my-Pal method in their congregational activities. I have received many assurances as to the effect of my message of individual responsibility. I am not anxious to found a great Society, but I am anxious to save society, and I am not anxious about the name, as long as the saving work is done.

When it was time for me to begin to make preparations to return to this country in January my wife was ill, and in her bed for some weeks. I told her I was going to cable to Pittsburgh and Toronto and Chicago to say I could not go on account of her illness. She would not hear of my staying at home. When I said that I could not think of leaving her in her bed, she said, "Certainly you must go to America. There is only one life at stake here, and there may be many lives at stake if you do not go out to your work. I cannot get better if you stay at home, for I'll be thinking all the time that it was on my account that you did not go away, and this thought will grieve me so that I cannot be well. But if you go I'll be getting such news of your work that I shall be encouraged to get better." When I still protested that I could not leave her, she said, "If you were the Captain of a ship in the Navy you'd have to go to fight for your country, even though I was ill. And if you were a common soldier in the ranks, you'd have to go out to kill men for the honor of your country and your king. But you are not being called out to kill men, but to save them, and surely you'll go for our KING." I felt that I could not resist that appeal, and it was with great heart tugging that I made up my mind to leave her. On the night of the 15th January I left Belfast to get the boat for Liverpool. My wife was so weak that she could hardly stand; yet she got up from her bed and dressed herself and came out on the stairs to say good-bye, as she did not want me to see her in her bed with my last look as I left her. I wonder if there are many women who would show such devotion to a good cause? I feel that, next to the inspiration I receive from Him Who loved me and gave Himself for me, I am inspired to go on with my work, even though four thousand miles from my delicate wife, by the splendid spirit of heroism she has shown, in counting not her life dear unto herself because she has such an intense desire to hear of the winning of the wanderers to a better life. And I feel that, believing in the God revealed in Jesus Christ, God cannot but bless my present visit to America, if it were only for the sake of that brave little woman in her bed in Belfast.

CHAPTER XXI

A Revival Jubilee

In the beginning of the year 1909, many earnest Christians in Ireland were praying for a revival to commemorate the Jubilee of the wonderful Year of Grace, 1859. Ministers were asked to preach special sermons on the subject. Prayer-meetings were held in many places over the land, and there was a great expectancy of a special answer to so much earnest prayer.

One night in a manse in County Derry I was sitting with three other ministers talking about the prospects of a revival. I ventured to say that I thought God would not signalise the jubilee of 1859 by a revival like the one in that year: that if a revival was coming, as I believed it was (for people were earnest in their prayers), it would be an ethical one: that people know the will of the Lord; that the revival would not take the form of a revelation of the Divine will, but would probably take that of *putting into more definite practice the will of God which people already know.* On my return home I said the same to a leading minister from Belfast, who was preaching in Armagh. He seemed to agree with me, and said he would mention some of these things at the prayer-meeting in Belfast the following day.

It was not long after these conversations that the Catch-my-Pal movement began. It showed many extraordinary spiritual signs, such as were expected by many who were praying for a revival; and it showed extraordinary activity in putting into practice

the principles of Good Samaritanship. No doubt, it
has been said that the movement swept over the country more like a religious than a temperance revival.
But it is both; only it recognises that the greatest bar-
rier to the chariot of God in the land is the drink evil,
and it grapples with it first. God's Spirit seems to in-
spire people with the thought that the drink demon
can be cast out in a more thorough-going way than
was formerly thought possible, and that it is for
them to take this opportunity by the forelock. Most
people have already realised that the drink is in the
way. The new thing, in which the revival manifests
itself, is the enthusiasm with which the people begin
to take the drink out of the way. This is their putting into more definite practice the will of God which
they already know.

*If the Catch-my-Pal movement is not the revival
God sent in answer to His praying people, it is ad-
mitted that no other revival was sent.* And those who
entered and are entering into the spirit of the movement, looking at it with their hearts' eyes and not
with the eyes of prejudice, freely admit that *it is a
revival indeed and in truth,* as many a fireside saved
from the curse and horrors of drink can testify.

*Sometimes conviction leads to action. This was the
note of the revival in* 1859. The leper knew he was
diseased, and cried out, "If Thou wilt Thou canst
make me clean." And Jesus said: "I will; be thou
clean." The leper's conviction of his own state and
of the power of Jesus to save him led him to take
action in asking for salvation.

In 1859 people became alarmed at their own sin-
ful state, and convinced of the power of Jesus to save.
They believed and were saved. Their conviction led
to action, the action of believing and asking for salvation.

*Sometimes action leads to conviction. This was the
note of the revival in* 1909. The man with the with-

ered hand was probably not thinking of Jesus being able to save him. He did not ask Him. He never would have thought of trying to use his hand. The case was, in his opinion, hopeless. But Jesus asked him to stretch out his hand, and the very action of stretching it out convinced him of the ability of Jesus to save and of his own ability to do, at the command of Jesus, what had seemed impossible.

In 1909 many helpless drinkers who thought they could never get on their feet again in a sober life heard a voice saying: "Stand upright on your feet!" And they stood upright, and are remaining so until this day, 1914, convinced of the power of Jesus to save them, and of their own ability, at His word, to do what seemed impossible.

CHAPTER XXII

DESPAIRING OF NO MAN

THE basal idea of the movement is that *every man and every woman is worth catching.* We therefore despair of no man and despair of no woman. Our desire is to save the biggest drinkers and greatest outcasts, as they are the ones whom Jesus would first seek out and save, seeing they need His salvation most.

I fear that far too often we assume many men and women want to go to the Devil, and we therefore do not trouble doing anything to save them. We look upon them as hopeless and let them go. Would it not be more in accordance with the mind of Jesus to assume the best regarding each human soul, to believe that everyone in his better moments wants to go to Heaven, *and would go if he got a chance?* In any case, whether our assumption proves right or wrong, *let every man have a chance.*

There are many jewels lying in life's dust heaps, which would prove a fortune to those who find them. Who is the man in the drunken gutter? He is a human soul,—a man lost for the finding, a man cast out for the bringing in, a diamond in the rough to be lifted, cut and polished, and made a thing of beauty and a joy for ever in the crown of Jesus Christ, the King of men. Who is that man there in the gutter? Your brother and mine. Why is he there? Very largely through his own fault, and also very largely through the fault of our modern civilisation. He has his own responsibility for being down, and *the community in which he fell has its responsibility.* And the

103

individuals who form the community have their individual responsibility, and it is largely through their fault the man is down so long. Catch-my-Palism asserts that it will pass no man and pass no woman by on life's highways, or down life's byways.

According to the rule of the motoring road every motorist, no matter how anxious he is to arrive at his destination, is called upon to slow down and have at least the courtesy to ask a fellow-motorist who has met with an accident: "Can I do anything to help you?" If he passes by with averted head and refuses to offer assistance, the stranded motorist would be justified in dubbing him "a mean scrub." The one on the roadside is just as anxious to arrive at his destination as the other who is passing by, but circumstances are against him. He needs a fellow traveller's hand to give him a fresh start; and having got it *he may outstrip even his helper* on the way. Many men and women are broken down in their moral and spiritual motor works. They are stranded on the way to heaven. They don't want to stay there. They would like to go on. They are just as anxious to go to heaven as the more fortunate ones who go regularly to church, attend all kinds of religious meetings, and pay so much attention to religious and ecclesiastical ritual as to show that they are tremendously in earnest to arrive at heaven's gates. But, if, in his earnestness to get to heaven, the churchgoer passes a fallen brother by, and if that fallen brother sees him pass by with arched Christian eyebrows, turned up nose, and curled lip, is it any wonder that he would dub his more fortunate brother as a "mean scrub"? Catch-my-Palism says: "I'll not arch my brow, or turn up my nose, or curl my lip, or turn away my face; I'll not pass by on the other side."

A lady is going along the street in her carriage. She happens to drop a valuable piece of jewelry with a diamond in it. As it falls its light flashes into the eyes of two gentlemen standing on the kerbstone. They see it sinking into the gutter at their feet. One pokes at it with his walking-stick and the other with his umbrella; but, *the more they try to poke it out, the more they poke it in.* They will not stoop to lift it with their fingers. They see the carriage stopping and the lady alighting. She comes to the place, takes off her gloves, and puts her fair white hand into the gutter. The thing is so precious to her that she gropes for it, and feels for it, and seeks it until she finds it. And when she has found it she rejoices more over that diamond than over all the other diamonds about her neck or in her jewel casket at home. Life's highways and byways are bestrewn with diamonds, fallen men and women and their children. *They are there for the lifting.* They make the greatest problem of our time. Many professing Christians, steady church-goers, are standing by life's way poking at the problem, not with walking-sticks or umbrellas, but with long, long, long tongues! They talk, and talk, and talk, and talk. *But talk never solved a social problem yet.* While men are talking God comes down from glory and becomes bone of our bone and flesh of our flesh at Bethlehem, and passes along the way bestrewn with diamonds in the mire. He comes to Calvary and there becomes sin of our sin, and plunges into the depths of human misery, debauchery, and sin, and feels after, and seeks after the lost till He has found. It was His glory to come into contact with the foulest of His day, and *the sweetest testimony ever given Him was that expressed in the most magnificent sneer that ever crossed human lips* when the self-righteous ones said: "This man receiveth the notorious sinners and is friendly with them," and in that name above every name, "the Friend of Sinners." It was the glory of the self-righteous persons to stand aloof and, gathering up their holy garments, whisk them out of the way when an outcast passed by; and what do the self-righteous of to-day in all our churches but just the same?

This is not an overdrawn statement of the case, if we simply modernize the parable of the Good Samaritan. The priest was the one from whom the man on the roadside might have expected most, and he proved to be the one from whom he received least. The Levite, from whom the half-dead one might have expected almost as much, gave almost as little. But the Samaritan, from whom he would have expected nothing, was the one who saw his case through by doing all he possibly could to save him. If we lay special emphasis on the word *and* in reading this parable, we shall see how clearly the characters of the three travellers along that highway are revealed. "And by chance there came down a certain priest that way; (1) *AND* when he saw him, he passed by on the other side. And likewise a Levite, when he was at the place, came (1) *AND* looked on him, (2) *AND* passed by on the other side. But a certain Samaritan, as he journeyed, came where he was: (1) *AND* when *he* saw him he had compassion on him, (2) *AND* went to him (3) *AND* bound up his wounds, pouring in oil and wine, (4) *AND* set him on his own beast, (5) AND brought him to an inn, (6) *AND* took care of him. (7) *AND* on the morrow when he was departing, he took out two pence, (8) *AND* gave them to the host, (9) *AND* said unto him: 'Take care of him; (10) *AND* whatsoever thou spendest more, when I come again I will repay thee.' " And our Lord says to each of us: "Go, and do thou likewise."

I have seen a picture representing the priest riding past the fallen man. The priest has his head turned away as if he were greatly engrossed with some object on the horizon on the other side, while the ass turns its head to look at the man in the ditch; the thought in the artist's mind evidently being that the beast had more concern for the fallen man than had the man who was on the beast's back. The man on the roadside did not want to lie there. He wanted to go on his journey, just as much as the priest or the Levite or the Samaritan, but he needed a chance, and the Samaritan gave it to him. It was a case of Catch-my-Palism. The Samaritan saw his opportunity; he said: "Here's a case for me, and I'll see this thing through." And he did.

A lady member of one of our branches told me the following story: "After the movement came into our town it was laid upon my heart to go and see a woman who was considered the most abandoned woman in the town, as far as drink was concerned. I thought it was quite useless to speak to her, and yet I felt constrained to speak. I went to her house and asked her to come to the meeting of the Union. She came and, to my surprise, she signed the pledge and kept it. She brought in her husband who was also a great drinker. He, too, signed and kept the pledge. They had five children who were half starved, and their fireside was almost like a pigsty. It is now two years since they signed, and now they have a well-furnished home, a well-spread table, and well-fed children around a happy fireside. Some time after I asked this woman to sign the pledge she met me, shook hands with me, and, with tears in her eyes and a tremor in her voice, she said: 'Thank you very much, Mrs., for your great kindness in speaking to me. *Many a time I was longing for someone to come and speak to me the way you did, but no one ever spoke to me but you.*'" She did not want to live in a hell here, and her life now shows that she did not want to go to a hell elsewhere. Catch-my-Palism gave her a chance by the hand of one in whose heart was the Spirit of Christ.

A man who had become so abandoned to drink that his town had given up all hope of his recovery was asked by a lady to go to the Catch-my-Pal meeting and take the pledge. He went and signed, but was in such a state of intoxication that the minister thought he did not know what he was doing. The minister brought him past all the saloons on his way home and, on arrival in his kitchen, saw two bottles of porter standing in the window. The minister asked the man to bring them to the door and smash them, but he said, "Let them alone, your reverence, let them alone." The minister then said, "You will take one bottle and I'll take the other, and each of us will smash a bottle." But he kept on saying "Let them alone, your reverence, let them alone. I'll fight them out; I'll fight them out." The minister went away and the two bottles remained. He expected to hear the next day that the man was drinking as usual, but found that he was quite sober. The bottles remained in the window and the man remained sober. He let them alone. He encamped round about them with a resolution of abstinence. He dug a trench about them that they could not pass over. He built a watch tower and "kept his eye on them." One day it seemed to him that they were holding a council of war as they stood in the sunlight watching him. Evidently they came to the conclusion that it was best to capitulate. They decided to throw up the sponge. *They burst!!!* They burst in the sunshine, and since that day there has been no dark shadow cast by drink over that fireside. That man, four years ago a seemingly hopeless drunkard, is now living the Christian life, a notable miracle of grace, a living surprise to all who know him.

One day when bathing on the County Dublin coast I lost control of myself and found myself sinking. I was the only person in the water at the time, but some young fellows were on the rocks after bathing. When I was just going under the water I threw up my hands and made signs of distress, and thought: "Surely I am not going to be drowned with those fellows there on the shore?" I lost consciousness almost immediately, and the next thing I knew was that I was recovering consciousness on the rocks. I asked who had saved me, and I was told it was Rex Clotworthy, a young student of Trinity College, Dublin. I went to his lodgings as soon as possible to try to express my gratitude. I asked him how he got me out. He said: "I was up on the path above the rocks, about to mount my bike to go home, when I heard a shout from the shore. I saw a pair of hands sinking in the water, and I said: 'There's someone in need of me!' I had on my waterproof and my hat and spectacles, and my bathing dress in one hand and a towel in the other. I dropped my bike, forgot to take off my hat and spectacles, forgot to drop the dress and towel, forgot about the waterproof, and I just rushed down and plunged in and had a great struggle with you in the water, and, with the help of others who waded into the water, I got you to the shore." I should be a craven soul if I did not put my friend, Rex Clotworthy, in the chief place of my heart's affection, nearest to my God and my own dearest ones, because of what he did for me. I did not want to be drowned that day. I wanted to be saved. My whole past life did not flash past me in a moment as is said to be the case with a drowning person. My last thought was of my wife and two boys, and it was for their sakes more than for my own that I longed for someone to save me.

At evangelistic and other meetings most church-going people are quite enthusiastic in singing: "Throw out the life-line, throw out the life-line, for some-one is sinking to-day," and *the only line that is thrown out in many cases is the line of the hymn!* But the line of the hymn is not a life-line, and it never saved anybody. At the sea-shore Rex Clotworthy did not stand to sing about a life-line. He did not throw out the line of a hymn. But God's angels surely heard heaven's harmonies struck out of the rocks by Clot-worthy's feet as he rushed to save a brother. He threw out the *life*-line, for, with all those encumbrances about him, he risked his life for me. He threw out *himself*. He put *himself* between me and death. He was *himself* the life-line. Can I ever express my gratitude to him? I wish I could think there was someone in the world who feels towards me as I do towards him. I should then know that I had not lived in vain, that it was a good thing to have been born.

I believe there are many of our fellows who are going down into drunkards' graves, who are yearning for salvation from the drink curse. And, perhaps, they are unselfish enough to yearn for it, not so much for their own sakes as for the sakes of those dependent on them. They feel, however, that circumstances are against them, and as they sink deeper and deeper in the evil habit I can well imagine that they are stretching out the hands of their souls and making signs of distress, and wondering: "Oh, is there none of these church-going people there on the rock of sobriety and professed Christianity who cares for my life? Is it nothing to all those who pass by that I sink into this hell? Is there no one to care for my soul?" I think many of this life's lost ones seem to have no thought for themselves because *no one else* takes thought for them; they have no respect for themselves because they think *no one else* respects them; they have no care for themselves because they think *no one else cares.*

The man at the pool of Bethesda was longing to be healed, and it was only when Jesus came that he got his chance; similarly *it is only when the spirit of Jesus shows itself in the actions of His professed followers that our fallen fellows will get their chance.*

I gave an address at a great meeting in England. At the close a young fellow came to the platform and began to speak up to me. I helped him to the platform as he was drunk. He gibbered to me, and it seemed as if the most of the great company roared out at him in laughter. I said: "Do you call yourselves Christians? Are you not ashamed of yourselves?

Who is this? He is your brother. Instead of laughing at him you should be sorrowful to think one of your brothers is in such a state. Laughing at a fallen brother! For one moment will you try to *imagine Jesus laughing at this man!*" The very thought of such an action on the part of Jesus seemed to cow that throng into silence and shame, and I appealed to them to put the arms of the town's brotherhood around that young man, and save him for a better life.

It was remarkable that at almost every one of my meetings at the beginning of the crusade a man under the influence of drink would be the first to come to the front to sign the pledge. And when such a man came forward I was often told that I should not give him the pledge.

It is impossible for me to keep in touch with the subsequent history of each person who signed in a state of intoxication; but I know of two who were considered hopeless cases, and who were living sober lives the last time I heard of them. One of them came up to me at the close of my appeal. He was so intoxicated that I asked him if he knew what he was doing. He said: "Yes, sir, I do know what I'm doing. I am the worst blackguard in the town." More than a year afterwards I saw that man in one of our great outdoor demonstrations. He had taken no drink in the interval, though he had been such a noted drinker that it was said of him that he had "drunk three fortunes," and might have been one of the richest men in his district.

At another meeting a man came up to me. He was so drunk that several persons, including two ministers, told me I should not give him the pledge. I said: "This is the man I am here for; this is the man for me." They tried to prevent me from pledging him, as they said he was the worst drinker in the town and did not know what he was doing. I helped him up on the platform and asked him his name. He told me. I'll

call him John. I addressed him by it, and asked him:
"Do you know what you are doing, John?"
"I do know what I am doin'."
"All right, old man, shake hands."
We shook hands. I said: "Look here, John, by the help of God, you'll be the best man in the town; won't you, John?"

He looked at me with his heavy eyes and said: "I'll try, your reverence."

It was most pathetic to hear that fallen son of God say, "I'll try." I patted him on the back and asked for three cheers for him. From that moment those who laughed at him became his brothers and sisters, and that outcast had the arms of the neighbourhood around him in Christian love and solicitude. Six months after that night a local minister told me that man was the best temperance worker in the town, and a year after, a young lady told me he was still staunch to his pledge.

Those who have been most vigorous in the Catch-my-Pal campaign have found that, on the average, the most notorious drinkers have been the quickest to respond to the call of brotherhood, and that *it is these drinkers who are keeping their pledges best.* If "joy shall be in heaven over one sinner that repenteth, more than over ninety and nine just persons who need no repentance," I am sure that there is joy in the presence of the angels of God over one of these reclaimed drunkards more than over ninety and nine respectable church-going people, who seem to need no repentance, and who seem to be thinking of nothing else but their own salvation.

I wish this movement to be known as *"A Good Samaritan of the Twentieth Century,"* that will pass no man and no woman by—*A SALVATION ARMY WITHIN THE CHURCHES.*

CHAPTER XXIII

Brands from the Burning

From all over the United Kingdom and many foreign parts I am constantly receiving word that drinkers who were considered to be hopeless cases four years ago are now living decent, sober, Christian lives. I here give a few testimonials which will show very clearly the sort of folk this movement is dealing with, and with what results. While Catch-my-Pal is not a Society of Reformed Drunkards, it is *a Society for reforming drunkards.*

* * * * * *

"A man left in comfortable circumstances by his father went completely to the bad through drink, and, losing everything, sank with his wife and large family to the depths of wretchedness and poverty. His wife was often compelled to stay out all night to escape his fury. He was frequently before the magistrates. On his own statement he thought nothing of spending a sovereign in a forenoon on drink. Catch-my-Pal got hold of him, and for nearly a year and a half he has been a stalwart in the total abstinence cause and interested to enthusiasm in the furtherance of the movement."

* * * * * *

"Two working men, with wives and families, were the greatest drunkards in this neighborhood. They have stuck to their pledge from the first, while others who were looked upon as moderate drinkers have broken their pledges."

* * * * * *

"In connection with our branch we have some very energetic members who, previous to their being 'caught,' were habitual callers in the saloons. One of these men in particular was down so far that his farm had become bare of stock and generally neglected. Instead of caring for it and making it pay, he spent any day he worked in the employment of his neighbours, I presume to get a few shillings in hand, which immediately went into 'liquidation.' There is now every prospect of things looking up for this man. Another young man, of a very cheerful, jovial disposition, was getting into the habit of having a 'good time' with a few kindred spirits every available evening; came under the influence of the movement; became a member, and has thrown himself heart and soul into the meetings, giving his musical and literary talents to the cause. He is a splendid asset in our fight with the drink. He has now a new outlook on life, which he is enjoying as he never did in his drinking days. A pal of this young man joined at the same time, and has proved to be an equally valuable member. His daily duties bring him into constant contact with children and young people, among whom his total abstinence principles are having a fine field of influence."

* * * * * * *

"We had one very bad case in this district, but I am glad to say he has kept his pledge from the beginning. His daughter states that he has done more work this year than he did for some years past."

* * * * * * *

"Amongst many cases of salvation from drink which I could name, I will content myself with one—that of a tradesman who, before the introduction of the movement, although earning over a pound a week, never had a penny to call his own. I fear his wife and family were very often hungry. He saw the error of his ways. He was one of the first caught by the Pal movement here, and has remained a faithful member up to the present, despite the jeers and laughs of his former companions. He is respected by every one except the local saloon keepers. He told me some time ago that he was better off than ever he was in his life, and that the desire to visit the pubs had clean gone."

* * * * * * *

"Our most noteworthy convert is a professional man whose home was broken up, and who became absolutely derelict. He has established his home again, and is now doing well and prospering."

* * * * * * *

"One case stands out very prominently. A skilled labourer, with a wife and family, spent practically all his earnings on drink. His clothing consisted of rags which he covered with an old overcoat when going to and from his work. He took the pledge fourteen months ago, and has kept it faithfully since, with the result that he and his family are now well dressed and attend church regularly. A young fellow, a farm servant, drank nearly all he earned. He took the pledge for twelve months, at the end of which time he was taken seriously ill. He thought some stimulants would do him good, so the old thirst was revived and he went on the spree for a short time. But he joined us again, and is now doing all right."

* * * * * * *

"The case we feel proudest of is that of a man whom everybody regarded as hopeless. He astonished us by coming to the meeting and taking the pledge. That was eighteen months ago, and he has not tasted a drink since. He says, 'anybody can quit drinkin' if he wants to.' He takes a great interest in the movement and has caught many pals."

* * * * * * *

"A respectable man, who never was quite sober for a month at a time, signed the pledge at the first meeting of our branch, and has kept the pledge ever since. A coachman, who had lost several good situations through drink and was working as a labourer, joined and kept the pledge faithfully. He attended the weekly meeting regularly. He has now got a good situation and has brought his family into our membership. A good tradesman who lost his situation through drink joined us over twelve months ago. He got another situation, and is now keeping strictly sober."

*   *   *   *   *   *   *

"A. B. joined at our first meeting. He had often been in *delirium tremens*. He is now a new man, and is doing a good business."

*   *   *   *   *   *   *

"S. W. was such a hopeless drunkard that for ten years he lived on his wife and children's earnings. We could never keep him at his work, although he was most skilful. He 'took the button' twenty months ago, and is now a changed man and an enthusiastic missionary. He is a bit of an orator, and is very helpful at our meetings."

*   *   *   *   *   *   *

"C. D. has gone into the neighbouring market for forty years, and was hardly ever known to come home sober. He joined the Union twenty months ago, and has not tasted drink since then."

*   *   *   *   *   *   *

"John —— earned good wages but spent it in the pub before he came home to his wife and two beautiful children. They had taken the total abstinence pledge and ceased not to pray for him. He joined our Union and has kept his pledge. He has been promoted to a very responsible position. I could multiply such cases."

*   *   *   *   *   *   *

"One of our members used never to be sober from Saturday night to Monday morning. His wife was even worse, as she was almost constantly dazed with drink. They had a squalid home, though thirty shillings of wages were earned weekly. The children were ragged and allowed to do as they pleased. One boy spent much of his time about the saloon, draining bottles and growing up to be the pest of the district. This man was one of the first to take the pledge. He was a surprise to many, and many unfavourable comments were made to the effect that he would never keep the pledge. The first evidences of reform were a new suit, his coming out to church, and his children coming to the Sabbath School. One boy has come to the Lord's Table. His wife is beginning to come to church. He is a member of our committee, a constant attender at public worship, and if we had no other case and no other reason for our existence as a temperance movement, this one alone should justify us in holding on to Catch-my-Palism."

*   *   *   *   *   *   *

"A man who was looked upon as almost hopeless, as he was almost constantly absent from work through his being stupid with drink, joined our branch and kept his pledge, although strongly tempted by his boon companions. He is very staunch, a member of committee, a splendid worker in bringing in new pals and backsliders, and one whose presence in our meeting is an inspiration to us all. He got a new suit when he joined, and he and his family now attend church most regularly."

*   *   *   *   *   *   *

"A hard drinker for many years, having lost more than one business through drink, was induced by the Church Army to sign the pledge at midnight on New Year's Eve. He had spent the whole day in a saloon. He joined the Catch-my-Pal the following week, bringing with him another hard drinker to sign at the same time. He has been working heart and soul in the Catch-my-Pal crusade ever since, and both are changed men, keen on winning others."

*   *   *   *   *   *   *

"We have a priest here who is deeply interested in temperance work and has been very successful among the Roman Catholics. Some time age he was lamenting to me the failures and shortcomings among those of his flock who had been won over to the great movement at the first, and said he was getting one of their accredited temperance priests to try and stir them up. 'But,' said he, 'I have been observing your people closely and can see what a great change is being wrought among them, and I believe they are keeping more strictly to their pledges than my people are."

* * * * * * *

"One man signed because the saloon keeper said he could not keep the pledge. He has kept it."

* * * * * * *

"There is a case of a young married woman which, I think, if the Catch-my-Pal movement had no other, would be worth all the trouble that has been taken. She was addicted to drink. I visited her and asked her to come to the Catch-my-Pal meeting. She tried to put me off, but as I was determined she said she would probably come after some weeks. I said that would not do, that I would come for her on Friday evening, that she was to be ready. But she would not let me come. 'Well, then,' I said, 'I am going to stay here till you promise to come. You will make me a cup of tea.' Finally she came, took the pledge, and has kept it ever since, although she has had some severe tests. I go to see her occasionally, and when I am from home I still have some little thing for her when I come back. It does not take much to please. A kind word goes a long way. This is one of many cases I could tell you about."

* * * * * * *

"A woman who was a great drinker and considered in every way *the most abandoned woman in the town* was brought into one of our meetings. She signed the pledge, and now, after more than four years, she is living a pure life, and goes about as a miracle of the Grace of God."

* * * * * * *

"The people of this district are nearly all mill-workers, and a few years ago it was considered the proper thing for men, when they left off work on 'pay Saturdays' to go straight to the saloons and sit drinking from quitting time till four or five o'clock, not going home for dinner. The apprentices and younger boys were encouraged and often forced to accompany the older men. This has practically all been changed. Very few men now go from their work to the public-house. They go home and have their dinner and clean themselves and go for a ramble through the country or attend a football match in season. Of course I do not mean to convey that all drinking has ceased, but even the men who do drink do not sit for hours in a saloon as they used to do. It is now considered most demeaning to be drunk. Some weeks ago there was a social meeting at which drink was served. Some of the older men became rather 'heady,' and I believe it was more or less of a race between those who did not drink to leave the building, fearing they would have to walk up the town in company with any of the persons who showed any sign of liquor. Not two years ago it was considered bad form to leave the same place unless in a state of intoxication. There are at least dozens of cases of most inveterate drinkers who have been saved from drink and become enthusiastic Catch-my-Pals. Two of these spent over $2,000 in drink in about four years. Another used to drink his entire pay, and make his daughter support the house with her earnings and keep him in clothes."

* * * * * * *

I could fill a large volume with records such as these I have given in this chapter. These are given that readers may see at a glance the kind of work this movement is doing among the drinkers in our land.

All kinds of folk have joined our ranks. Men and women in almost every class of society have been rescued. I know doctors, solicitors, ministers, business men of all kinds, ladies of high standing as well as those of low degree, who have been lifted up out of drink by the hand of Catch-my-Pal, as an instrument of the Grace of God.

CHAPTER XXIV

A Typical Report from a Branch Secretary

"So popular has the Catch-my-Pal Society become in our town that we have all sorts and conditions of men, women and children asking our aid for fallen brothers and sisters. We have had wonderful cases of redemption brought about by an 'unseen' power which makes us feel God is working with us and by us.

"Late one Saturday night, between eleven o'clock and twelve o'clock, I heard a timid knock at my door. I found two children, a boy of twelve years and a girl of four, on my doorstep. I brought them into the light. They were well clothed and well nourished, but scared and frightened. They said their father and mother were drunk and that the mother had been striking the girl. The boy sobbed in a heartbreaking way. When he had got some relief he told me he had come to me as he heard I had something to do with drunk people. My wife and I gave the little things supper and put them to bed, and then went to enquire about the parents. When we came to their house, which was in a very respectable quarter of the town, the door was opened by a drunken woman. We asked for her husband. She said he was in bed, drunk. We asked about their children, and she broke into an awful tirade against them, threatening what she would do to them when they came home. We came away and went to the police barracks, and told an officer that the children were with us. On Sunday morning I answered a knock at my door, and found the children's father on the step. A more dejected man I never saw. He gasped, 'Are they here?' I said they were, and he explained how he had walked the streets since four o'clock looking for them. He was told by the police that they were safe, but that he would not be informed where they were till nine o'clock. I said he would get the children back on condition he would join the Catch-my-Pal society. He said he would do anything, for he never would be in such a plight again. I arranged to visit his home in the afternoon. I went and found the wife a poor victim of alcoholism, so much so that her mind was deranged. She had been in an asylum, but was permitted to return home. She went back among her old companions, the forenoon drinkers, who spend their time in lazy gossip while their husbands are at work. One of the children had died in hospital, and the husband lost heart and took to drink to drown his sorrow. Things became worse and worse till the incident of the two children called him to a halt.

"I brought a Catch-my-Pal card and button with me. He signed the pledge and put on the button. I asked him to come to the next meeting of our branch and make a public declaration of his having signed the pledge. He did so, and has faithfully kept the pledge since. The little girl comes very often to my home. It is very sad to see the father doing everything in the house. He washes, bakes, keeps the house in order, puts the girlie's hair in curls every night, and then puts her to bed. The mother is a wreck through drink.

"At one of our meetings I told a story of a drunken man buying damaged fruit to bring home to his children. That night a man signed the pledge. I met him about two months after, and he asked me who told me about his buying rotten fruit for the children. I said I did not speak about him at all, but of another man. He had been spending his money in drink, and brought home damaged fruit to his children, so he took to heart what I had said and signed the pledge. He has kept the pledge faithfully, and told me he has now ham and eggs for his breakfast.

"A mother came with tears in her eyes, and, with a torn heart, she began to plead for our aid for her son who had gone headlong into the abyss of drink since the death of his father three months before. He was a good fellow, but easily led. We went to him and asked him to come and help us, as he would be of great use to us in saving others from drink. He signed the pledge and is now one of our most active workers.

"A father and mother in a respectable class, whose daughter was led astray and began to walk the streets at an early age, came to us and asked us to intercede with her and lead her to a proper life. We found her in jail and brought her to an hospital, and afterwards to a home, where she could work out her salvation, and in a year or so be so trained that she could go to a situation far from the haunts of those she knew.

"We have had striking success in being the means of saving several poor fallen women who have tried over and over again to begin a new life.

"That the Catch-my-Pal society is doing good work is proved by the reports of foremen in our large public works. Men who were formerly off work through drink are now constant at the bench. Each man has in his coat the little white and blue button, the charm of his life.

"One poor fellow came and joined our society. The next morning he was terribly burnt in the pit and died in the afternoon. The Catch-my-Pal society interested themselves in the widow and children, and are now trustees in dispensing the money received as compensation. The sheriff remarked that she would be better looked after by our society than otherwise.

"A bright little mother glowed with pride as she said,'*Last New Year was the first my husband ever spent with me and the children.'* They all came to the Pal soirée, well dressed and happy.

"On going to my business one morning a very respectable shopkeeper stopped me and told me about his brother, who had a wife and four children and was bringing them to ruin through drink. After a hard battle we got him to join the society. Though he fell once, we got him on the rebound. He is now a staunch member of the society and was at your meeting the last time you were in our town.

"There are many interesting incidents that have come under the notice of other members of the society. I send you these which have come under my own notice, and if you can make any use of them you are at liberty to do so."

*   *   *   *   *   *   *

Such is the record of one branch secretary. Many such records come to me from all parts of the country.

Down in the human heart, crushed by the tempter,
  Feelings lie buried that grace can restore;
Touched by a loving hand, wakened by kindness,
  Chords that were broken will vibrate once more.

CHAPTER XXV

Two Scotch Pals

At a great Unionist demonstration in Belfast on Easter Tuesday, 1912, a man came to me and said, "I have been watching you for some time, and I was determined not to go away without speaking to you." I did not know the man and I asked him why he wanted to speak to me. He said his name was Law and that he was at the first meeting I addressed in Scotland at Bellshill. I asked him if he had joined the Union. He said he had, and that he had great need to do so. He did not appear to me to be a man who had been accustomed at any time to take drink.

Almost every place I visit, where Catch-my-Pal work has been in progress, *I meet men and women who were formerly slaves of drink, but who are now so much reformed that no traces of their old life are seen upon them.* One evening I sat down to supper after a meeting and enjoyed conversation with the friends around the table. When they went away my host told me something of the histories of three of them. I was much surprised to find that they had been addicted to drink and had been led to give it up through the Pal movement. No one would ever have suspected those three of having been heavy drinkers. At a meeting in a Presbyterian Church in County Derry I was struck by the great interest shown in the arrangements by one man in particular. I thanked him for his help, and he told me how he had been a great drinker and had been saved through the movement. At the close of the same meeting I was addressed by one whom I considered to be an elder of the Church. He told me how he had been one of the hardest drinkers in the neighbourhood and had been delivered from the curse. "And," said his wife who was at his side, "no one knows the change that has come over him better than I." "Why," I said, "your good man looks so respectable *I thought he was one of the elders!*"

I asked Mr. Law if any good work was being done at Bellshill, and if there were any outstanding cases of reform. He said he would send me some information when he went back to Bellshill. He requested the Rev. Daniel M'Iver, minister of the Evangelical Union Church, Bellshill, to communicate with me, and I have permission to publish his communication:

"In the summer of 1909 I came to the conclusion, after a few months' work among the ironworkers and miners of Bellshill and district, that something more than purely evangelistic effort was required in order to get at the many drinkers hereabout. Scores of men might possibly listen to the temperance appeal, I thought, when they would not listen to the purely evangelistic; and many would come to a meeting of a social nature who would not venture to a purely religious gathering. And so while I was discussing the matter with my office bearers it eventually turned out that you were going ahead in Ireland with your campaign. This I discovered by the article which appeared in *The Glasgow Herald* in the month of November, 1909, in which a full and informative statement of your good work was made known to Scottish readers. 'Here,' I said, 'is my idea carried out in a manner far better than I could have devised.'

"*The discovery of your work was made the basis of future action on my part.* I called a public meeting, at which only eleven men responded when requested to take the pledge. We formed ourselves into a Union on the lines of your own great effort, and I was made the president.

"But the work suddenly sprang into favour, and we noticed in a Glasgow paper that you were to address a meeting of the Palace P.S.A., Glasgow, on Sunday, 2nd January, 1910. As the result of correspondence you addressed your first Catch-my-Pal meeting in Scotland at Bellshill on Thursday, 30th December, 1909. The minister of the parish was in the chair and every minister in the town was on the platform.

"The meeting was a great success, all present being raised to the highest pitch of enthusiasm, with the result that sixty-five men and twenty-eight women signed the pledge. That was the first of a succession of good catches. The meetings are still continued with great enthusiasm, and the membership reaches up to hundreds.

"I relinquished the presidentship about eighteen months ago, in order to get Mr. Charles Law into full harness; for this good man had not long been a member before it was borne in upon me that the future of Catch-my-Pal in Bellshill, under God, depended upon Charlie Law. Somewhat under forty, a favourite with most men, and the best of company, his conversion to Catch-my-Pal has had great and important results, *scores of men having been won by his enthusiasm.* He heard you lecture, but would not sign then. His wife, however, had stood up with the others at your meeting —an action which brought the blush of shame to her husband's cheek, especially as she had no need to take the pledge for her own sake. Law left the meeting unhappy. Next day mentally he continued to debate the matter at work, and as he made his way home, he was met by a chum who said: 'Come on, Charlie, and let us have a drink.' Law answered: 'No, I'm not going. I was at the Catch-my-Pal meeting last night in the E.U. Church, and heard that Mr. Patterson from Ireland, and was never so much impressed in my life, and I have made up my mind to-day that I'll have no more to do with it. You,' he added,

THE HAPPY ART OF CATCHING MEN

'would be well advised if you gave it up too.' They got past the saloon. That was temptation number one; and it was no easy thing to muster courage to pass a drink-shop into which he had been accustomed to go daily for years.

"Temptation number two awaited him at home. In order to keep him out of the pub Mrs. Law got the brewer to send occasionally some bottles of beer to the house. Mr. Law was supposed to drink one before dinner in lieu of the glass of whisky he would have had at the pub, every day, had he gone in! 'But,' he says, 'my wife was deceived, for instead of passing the pub, as she supposed I did, I went in and had my whisky, and then when I arrived home I took away the smell of it by drinking a bottle of beer.' Well, upon arrival home that day, he found the brewer's dray was at the door, and the boy had delivered the usual order. What was to be done? 'Minnie,' said he to his wife, 'tell that man to take back the beer; and if he fears trouble, give him a shilling and I'll pay for the whole thing. But it's not coming in here.' Temptation number two was overcome—all on 31st December, 1909, and he had the New Year holidays to face!

"On the 8th January, 1910, Mr. Law signed the Catch-my-Pal pledge at a meeting of the Union in my church. It was a great social event, for it meant a very great deal to a man so popular. Generous to a fault, he was the centre of an influential social circle, and on all hands and at every turn he was met with temptation. His most intimate friends were saloon-keepers and frequenters of saloons; this being so he was as a man utterly deserted, for his new attitude to the drink question was the signal to scatter on the part of many who would have held fast to him had he not joined the Union.

"A manly man, keenly interested in all manly games, Mr. Law had many friends also amongst the leading football enthusiasts of Scotland. When at the International match in Glasgow, April, 1910, he was met by an outstanding football enthusiast, who said: 'Come away, Charlie, and have a drink for old time's sake.' 'I'm sorry,' he replied, 'but this wee button comes between me and the saloon.' The enthusiast slapped him on the back saying: 'Quite right, Charlie; stick to it!' That too from a popular traveller for a firm of whisky merchants!

"Mr. Law frequently represents his fellow workmen at the conferences between the masters and representatives of the Iron-workers' Union. At the conclusion of one of these conferences he found himself the odd man in a company of four, and declined to enter the pub. At last, at a railway junction on the way from this conference, which was held in an English city, he was appealed to not to break the company, that he could enter the pub, and have a temperance refreshment. He considered so far that he crossed the street towards the inn; but when he got to the door he drew himself up saying: 'No, I won't! It would make me weak.' And so he obtained the victory.

"Mr. Law is now the president of the Bellshill Catch-my-Pal Union. He has been enabled to capture for the cause many noted drinkers. He appeals to men at all times and under all circumstances. A forceful speaker, he can use the experience of his former days in a manner that reveals the sincerity of the man. Neither vain nor boastful he will give his testimony believing that while there is much that makes him feel ashamed, there is also much in it that can help others who have been what he once was. Day and night he works for Catch-my-Pal, and if Catch-my-Pal had done no more in Bellshill than win Charlie Law it would have justified its existence. Devoutly grateful for the Union, he sees, in his own case, that it has been the instrument of God. 'I believe,' he will say with the tear in his eye, 'that prayers of my dear old father and mother, now at rest, are being fulfilled in my experience.'

"With nothing namby-pamby about him, Mr. Law gives a testimony that impresses because of its clear religious note. When pledging a man under very strange circumstances, Mr. Law got him to hold up his hand while he would repeat the well-known words. But the president just got 'For God and Home and Native Land' spoken, when the man lowered his hand saying: *'No; not for God.'* (Poor chap, he had lost faith in some Christian people, and so was losing faith in God.) 'Well,' answered Mr. Law, 'I can go no further with you; for I could not have fought and obtained the victory but for God, and neither will you. I have no hope apart from God's grace, and I refuse to pledge you.' The man was won and is a testimony to the great, if unconventional, work of Charlie Law. It is a work of God and the man is a token of God's grace. He is a wonder to himself, much more so than to the world."

*   *   *   *   *   *   *

Mr. M'Iver sends me the following speech, given by Thomas Stewart at a meeting in Bellshill in November, 1911:

"Mr. Law won't give me peace; he says I must give the promised speech. Well, here it is, and I'll give you a wee bit of history:—

"Many folk think I was born in Scotland, but I was not; I was born in County Antrim. Leaving Antrim in 1872, I came to Motherwell. For a time all went well, but after my father's death I thought of going to America. I was a decent chap then, getting certificates of character from my minister and employer which testified to my sobriety and steadiness. But I never got to America yet. If I had gone, perhaps my history would have been better. At any rate, by staying in this country I was introduced to the liquor trade; I got to know all the ins and outs of the business, for I stood at ——'s saloon bar in Motherwell for a number of years. After serious trouble in my home life I began to take a 'drap on the sly.' Lodgings were uncomfortable, and housekeepers did not make a home. I took more drink than was good for me, and when I saw that the habit was eating in on me, I went to my master and said: 'I'm going to leave.' The publican would not hear of such a thing; he expressed himself as well satisfied with my conduct of the business; the drawings had increased, and he saw no reason why, if I wanted it, I should not take a 'drap' on the quiet, without letting anyone know about it. Well, I left him.

"Starting in Mossend Ironworks, I was knocked about in lodgings for seventeen years, having land-ladies good and bad during that time. In one house the landlord would be drunk on Saturdays; so would another lodger; while, I am sorry to have to confess it, I would be drunk six nights in the week and twice on Sundays.

"In 1893 I was in the Royal Infirmary, Glasgow, through drink, upon two occasions. I went astray on a Saturday night, and when I came to myself on Monday morning, I thought I was in Govan, but it was Rutherglen. My pockets were empty, although I had a big pay in them that day. Three Bellshill men had rifled them in my helplessness. I got up in a dazed condition; shivering with cold and bare-headed, I ploughed my way in the dark, crossed a burn, and made my way round an unprotected pit mouth. It was a wonder I escaped death, for I fell down the hill-face. That meant a month in the Royal Infirmary.

"I started work again, and in 1899 things were going very fair, but I fell back once more. However, I still commanded some respect, for I got married at this time. Unfortunately the night after my marriage I got the sack, and I walked about for seventeen weeks. Not a bad start in double harness! Before I was restored to Mossend works I got a job at carting. But again I was thrown out, having no one to blame but myself. Now this was a trying period for my wife. A drinking man is a troublesome man, and knowing his own weakness, he does not like his wife not to share in his drinking ways. In this sort of temper a man will do and say things that he would not in his sober senses, and many a woman may take a glass just to please her husband, just to keep the peace. But my wife was strong against my drinking, and as a consequence she had to suffer a man who thought nothing of what he spent in this way. And drink will make a man do shameful things. He will take a $15 suit to the pawn, although he may get no more than $4 on it; or a $12 watch, on which he may get no more than $5. But I had better draw the curtain between my doings and this audience.

"However, a turning point was at last reached. And this is how it happened. In October, 1909, when at Mrs. F.'s garden, this good lady said: 'Tom, you're smelling of drink. Now you can't come here in that state.' Well, I did not go again to her house until after the New Year, when Mrs. F. said: 'Ah, Tom, you will need to go to the Catch-my-Pal. Mr. Law joined the other Saturday; you must come too.' I was going into drink very heavily. I said to myself, 'This is not going to do. I'll take Mrs. F.'s advice.' My good friend, this Christian lady, said she would be happy to accompany me. On 12th February, 1910, I signed the pledge in the E.U. Kirk; so also did my wife, and the two of us have kept faithful to the cause ever since.

"I would like to say how much the meetings mean to me; and I thank God for the Catch-my-Pal Total Abstinence Union."

*   *   *   *   *   *   *

"Mr. Stewart does not mind saying that he used to be known as 'Drunken Stewart.' He is a most enthusiastic member of the Union, and is quite a brand plucked from the burning. When he joined he was pretty well weighted with drink, how much he had taken I cannot at this date tell; but I said to myself as I smelt his breath: 'That poor chap won't hold out long.' But there he is—clothed and in his right mind, a regular worshipper in the Established Church, a credit to the Catch-my-Pal, and, I believe, a glory to God."

I was in Bellshill in November, 1912. Mr. Law presided at the meeting. At its close he asked me to go down to his house. I went and saw his happy wife. He and Tom Stewart presented me with a lovely gold-mounted umbrella, as a token of their love, and as an appreciation of what Catch-my-Pal had done for them.

Again, in November, 1913, I was in Bellshill, and stayed for the week end with Mr. Law. He brought me to Tom Stewart's house, which is now spotlessly clean and beautifully furnished, his wife being a picture of happiness. He told me how his house was a "dirty hut" four years ago. As we went to the meeting together Tom said to me, "Sometimes when I think of what I was, and of what I now am, if the thought comes into my head of going back to the drink again, I just look up to God and the spirit of the men of Londonderry comes into me and I just pull myself together and I say, 'No Surrender.'"

I walked down the main street of Bellshill after Divine Service on Sunday morning with Charlie Law on one side, and Tom Stewart on the other. I think there was not a happier minister in Scotland that day, as those two men gave me their testimony; and Stewart acknowledged he was now God's child in Christ. Law is now about the busiest Christian worker in Bellshill. As for drink, he says, "I simply *can't* go back to it. I can't go back."

At the recent election for the Parish Council Mr. Law was returned at the top of the poll.

CHAPTER XXVI

An Irish Pal's Story

MANY men who have been rescued from drink by this movement are now devoting much of their time to addressing meetings and helping the cause in other ways. One of them, Mr. Joseph Kane, Belfast, has been doing splendid work in that city and in other towns to which he has been invited to speak. His is a typical case, and I am sure my readers would like to read his own testimony. He says:

"If anyone wants to know what the Catch-my-Pal movement can do in the hand of God for a man's salvation, I am not ashamed to tell my story. In the year 1909, in the month of December, I was as low down as I could get, away from my wife and family, naked, miserable, wretched. In fact I was not fit to live, and I was not ready to die. If I were to give you the history of my life from the first time I took drink you would need to write another book. But I'll give you just a smattering of what I have come through. It would take another book to tell all the blessing I and my wife and family have had since I joined the Catch-my-Pals.

"A few weeks before I joined I got such a feed of drink in a bonded warehouse that I was picked up unconscious in the street, and taken to the police office. This was about *my sixteenth turn in the barracks, all through drink*. The doctor ordered my removal to the union infirmary that I might be pumped. I was taken on the following day to the police office in a patrol van, for they are so careful they would not let you walk, I was brought before the magistrate who gave me a sound castigation, and said he would let me off if I took the pledge. Well, I had seven 'browns,' which mean fourteen cents, and as I was dying for a drink I gave the promise, I took the pledge, but I would at the same time have taken a hundred pledges to get out for another drink. Five minutes afterwards I had three pints of porter, and then I went in for another big bout.

"Some days after this I was asked to go to a meeting of the Catch-my-Pal society. *My experience is that there are quite a lot of fellows who are only waiting to be asked to give up the drink.* The night I went to the meeting I had eight pints of stout. That was on the 13th December, 1909, and I thank God I have kept my vow since, and with His help I mean to keep it till my dying day.

"Some people wag their heads and say that if a man is 'saved' there is no need for him to take the pledge. I say the same; but you must remember that if you preach salvation to a man in a drunken state he will pay no attention. Get him to be sober, and then he begins to look for something better than drink. He will likely go to church as I did, and be led to know Christ as I was led. Before I signed the pledge I had no desire for anything but drink. Now my whole desire is to serve the Lord and do what I can for Him.

"Since I joined the Catch-my-Pals I have addressed many meetings, especially in the open air. I believe in open air work. I have met some wonderful fellows at these meetings. Now, what appeals more to a poor drunkard than one of his own class standing up and giving testimony, and not keeping anything back? My advice to pals who have been lifted out of the gutter is to beware of becoming proud when you are well dressed, because if you become proud you are in a very shaky place. I was speaking at an open air meeting one night, and I noticed how the chaps were watching every move of the speakers. They had criticised the previous speaker. who was a temperance orator. One fellow says: 'Oh, he is making a fine thing out of it.' Another says: 'What do you know about the power of drink?' And the speaker had to admit that he knew very little about it. I was the next to mount the platform. Indeed, to all appearance I was as great a 'knob' as the previous speaker as far as clothes go. Then you should have seen the stir among the critics. I said: 'My brothers, it is not long since the worst looking man in this crowd was a better dressed man than I was. Some of you have at least a coat. Well I could say I had not half a coat. Because if I had anything that they would take in the pawn, it would have gone there and old subs and relievers would have taken its place.' After telling this I got as good a reception as any man ever got from a crowd. They listened to me with the greatest attention, and some of them promised to try and do better.

"A chap who joined my branch is doing well in America now. He sent a letter home lately and inquired how the Rev. Joseph Kane was doing! That was my humble self, if you please, and I suppose he thought the title was good enough for me!

"At a meeting I was addressing a fellow kept on asking about Home Rule. Some were for putting him away from the meeting, but I suggested that it was better that he should be there annoying us than annoying his wife and children at home. He was quiet all the rest of the meeting, and he took the pledge later on. Another man came to my own home one night. Of course I wondered what he could want with me, as at one period of his life he held a good position in Belfast. Well, he said, he had been watching me for a long time and he came to me to take the pledge. Poor fellow, he was trying to keep respectable, but found he was almost beat. He took the pledge and joined my branch, and, as far as I know, is living a sober life.

"Men have come to me and said: 'I wish to God I could keep sober like you.' My answer is: 'Do you want to live a sober life? Then give yourself into God's keeping and try Him. When He can keep me surely He can keep you also.' The worst of them can never get the better of me in giving excuses for not giving up the drink, for I was as low as ever a man could be, and I know all about the drunken life and the temptations the drinker has to meet. One chap said to me at a meeting:

" 'You say you have experienced a great many curious places in your day. Well, you don't look it. Did you ever live in a model lodging house?'

" 'Yes, and in a thruppenny bed to boot.'

" 'Were you ever in jail?'

" 'Yes, often, but it was for being drunk and disorderly.'

" 'Did you ever sleep with the sky for a roof?'

" 'Yes, indeed, I have. I used to pay a carman by the week to drive me home from a certain pub every night as I was not fit to walk. Some nights he arrived at my door with his car and *I was not on it!* I had rolled off, and he did not know it as he had too much drink himself. One night I was so drunk I wandered into a place where a new house was being built. I lay down in the mud and felt it so soft I thought I was in bed. When I woke in the morning and looked up and saw the sky I found I was not in bed. Such a sight as I was after rolling about in the mud all night! Yes, I *have* slept with the sky for a roof. Have you any more questions?'

"He replied by giving me a shake of the hand and saying: 'I believe you are a genuine chap.'

"At another meeting a poor fellow came along drunk. He began to obstruct the meeting. He annoyed the speaker very much. When the chairman asked me to get up, I said to the drunk fellow: 'I want you to keep quiet till I am done; then I'll hear you.' I appealed to the people and said: 'Twenty-seven months ago I was a worse case than this poor chap before you to-night.' He looked up at what you would call a well-dressed man, for since I joined the Pals I have got plenty of good clothes. He said: 'You are a liar!' He kept quiet till the end of the meeting, and then I brought him and three or four others into the hall where they signed the pledge.

"It is a pity that people will not subscribe more to help work like what the Pals are doing. If the philanthropic men of the country knew as much as I know. about men who have been lifted up out of the gutter by the movement, they would take a deeper interest in our work."

*   *   *   *   *   *   *

This man, Joe Kane, is now engaged by our Executive Committee as a Temperance Missionary. He is a man of great natural ability and considerable oratorical power. He has been the means of rescuing great numbers of the "down-and-outs" all over the north of Ireland, and in some places in Scotland.

If some American millionaire would supply us with the necessary funds *we could put several men like Kane in the field* to go out to appeal, as no ministers could, to the drunkards to come into the sober life. May I hope that some good American heart may be touched by the story in this book, and be led to consecrate some money to the saving of the drunkards, many, many of whom are longing to be saved from drink *if there was only someone to come and save them?*

CHAPTER XXVII

Why Did the Child Fall Down the Stairs?

SUPERFICIAL critics and unsympathetic observers of this movement have been pointing their fingers of scorn at it because many of those who have signed the Catch-my-Pal pledge have not been faithful to it. He would be a silly reformer who expected all persons who rally to his standard to be true and faithful.

On the night before the Crucifixion of our Lord eleven men took a solemn pledge. Peter said: "Even if I must die with Thee yet I will not deny Thee." This was a pledge. It was taken by the eleven. "Likewise also said all the disciples." How long did they keep it? Not for a single night. But perhaps Peter did not know what he said, or wist not what to say, as when he was on the mount of transfiguration. In any case, *Peter was the arch-pledge-taker and he became the arch-pledge-breaker.* Peter followed afar off. All the disciples forsook Him and fled. Peter cursed and swore that he did not know Jesus. What a horrible pit Peter digged for himself that early morning in the courtyard! He was plunging into it as Jesus passed out between the soldiers.

How did Jesus treat the pledge-breaker? Not as cynical and superior persons treat those who break the temperance pledge. "The Lord turned and looked upon Peter." What kind of a look was that? Was it a look of scorn, or of contempt, or of despair? Was it a look that made Peter feel the Lord would trample upon him when he was down? Or was it a look of disappointed love, a look that made Peter hear as well as see; that made him hear the heart that looked through those Divine eyes? Did not Peter hear that heart *speak through a look,* as there was no opportunity for it to express itself to him in speech? And what did Peter hear that heart say as the Eyes turned on him? Was it not something like this? "Ah, Simon, thou art not the Rock Man yet. Satan still desires to have thee. Thou art being sifted this morning as wheat. I know what thou hast said about Me. I have prayed the Father for thee. I do not despair of thee. Circumstances are hard. I'll have thee back yet. Stand up, Simon. Try again! I shall see thee yet as the Man of Rock at My side."

And "Peter went out and wept bitterly." Why? Because not even his cursing and swearing could stem the love of Jesus, and because he felt that long-suffering love was giving him another chance. Long-suffering led him to repentance. *The magic of another chance* distilled him into tears. He came up out of the horrible pit only to find himself in the maelstrom of Divine love. That love that hoped all things washed him and cleansed him, revived him, converted him, and changed him from Simon, son of Jonas, who denied his Lord, into the Rock Man Peter, who turned and looked upon Jesus with a look of such intense yearning as perhaps Jesus never saw in the face of any other man. As their eyes met that day by the lakeside Peter did not need to ask if *Jesus* loved *him,* but his heart must have well-nigh burst as he tried to say: "Yea, Lord, Thou knowest all things; Thou knowest that *I* love *Thee.*"

If there is life in a look *at* the Crucified One, there is also life in the look *of* the Crucified One. Oh, that all who profess to follow in His steps along life's ways brought His look of sympathy, hope and long-suffering, with them! *How our fallen brothers and sisters would leap up to God if they could only read in our eyes that there was hope for them yet!*

"Why did my child fall down the stairs?" Will

you, if you are a parent, ask yourself this question?
What answer do you give to it? Think for a moment.
"Why did my child fall down the stairs?" *Because
he was up.* If he had not been up, he could not have
fallen down. How often shall I run to lift up my
fallen child? Just as often as he falls. I put my
hand under his chin. I become the lifter up of his
head. I tell him he must be more careful, and I give
him advice; but with all my advice and caution I mix
sympathy and watchfulness and long-suffering, until
I see that my child's head has become steady, and his
feet and ankle bones have received enough strength
to enable him to go up the stairs as surely as myself.
I taught him to say:

> "If at first you don't succeed,
> Try, try, try again."

and I let him see that I had patience with him while
he tried.

Why do many of those who sign the pledge of this
and other similar movements fall? Just because they
were up. If they had lain in the gutter all the time
the cynic would have passed no remark about them
but would simply have passed by on the other side.
But when they take the pledge and rise a little they
become the curiosity of their neighbourhood. The
miserable cynic did nothing to lift them up and does
nothing to keep them up, but is ever ready like a car-
rion fly to pounce upon them when they fall.

The poor inebriate falls because he was like a child
on the stairs. His will power is almost gone. His
very elevation from the gutter for even a short time
makes him giddy. He has not yet learned what that
meaneth: "Let him that thinketh he standeth take
heed lest he fall." He will probably fall again and
again. But *it is for the Christian community about
him to be a mother to him in his weakness;* to run
and lift him again and again, and put him again and

again on the first step of life's stairs and encourage him from step to step and from strength to strength, till that son of the gutter begins to feel within himself that he is of such stuff as men·are made of by the Grace of God extended to them by the hand of human sympathy and long-suffering. Then he will mount up with steady steps and not cease mounting till he goes in among the spirits of just men made perfect.

Our Lord said to the apostles, "If thy brother trespass against thee rebuke him; and if he repent forgive him. And if he trespass against thee seven times in a day, and seven times in a day turn again to thee saying, I repent; thou shalt forgive him." And what did the apostles say? "Lord, Increase Our Faith." Increase our faith in the goodness of God, Who would forgive so often; and increase our faith in our falling fellows, that we may have hope that the worst of them may be finally saved even after uncountable falls.

Christianity is not dead though "all the disciples forsook Him and fled." They all came back, and *eleven cowards became the finest team that ever went out to do battle with the legions of darkness.* One of the most hopeful signs of the permanency of this movement is the readiness with which those who break the pledge come back to renew it, and the spirit of hopefulness that broods over the most reckless cases, nursing them gradually back to self-reliance through the love of God and human brotherhood. And many of the most valiant workers for God and Home and Country in the ranks of the Catch-my-Pal to-day are men and women who had to be lifted up again and again before they found strength to stand on their feet. While they make progress on life's highway the movement need not fear the hissing of the cynic who stands behind the hedge. Notorious drunkards and harlots who, in God's great mercy, have been saved by the Catch-my-Pal crusade, will go into the kingdom of God before the cynic.

CHAPTER XXVIII

The Man Behind the Bar: Before Whose Bar Does He Stand?

One characteristic of this movement is that its heralds have not tried to make capital for temperance reform by *hammering the heads of the saloon-keepers.* We have reason to believe there are "black sheep in every flock." There are black sheep in the ministry. We find them among grocers, drapers, watchmakers, bakers, plumbers, and behind every kind of counter and in every sort of office. There are many persons engaged in the drink trade who really do not care how many lives are lost as long as they make money. But there are many persons engaged in the trade who are decent, respectable and honest, and who conduct the business in as decent, respectable, and honest a manner as it is possible for such a business to be conducted. I have had as much to do with saloon men in the course of my ministry as perhaps any other man in Ireland at any rate. I have often been surprised at the thoughts I have heard expressed by those in the trade. I have heard a dying saloon-keeper say to me: "If I had to begin my life over again I would have nothing whatever to do with the business." He asked me to use my influence to keep young men from going into it, and I am grateful to be able to say that I have been instrumental in turning some from taking that *black path to fortune.*

I think I can truthfully say that I never attacked saloon-keepers from the pulpit. I did not think it was a manly thing to attack a man from the pulpit when he had no right to reply from the pew. I considered it a more manly part to go into a man's own house or bar, and to try to square him up there. We could give one another tit for tat there, while if I attacked him from the pulpit it was *all tit and no tat.* But I considered it to be my duty in the pulpit to describe in the most vivid and lurid terms the evil results of drink as I had seen them in the human body, and in the human soul, in family and in national history. I preached in such terms very often, and I called my discourses "squirming sermons." I called to see a wine-merchant one Monday after a squirming sermon. He said to me in his bar:

"That was a good sermon you gave us yesterday." I thought he was making fun of me, and I said:

"I am surprised to hear *you* say that."

"You ought to publish that sermon," he continued.

"Why, what do you mean?" I asked.

"Just what I say. I think you ought to publish that sermon. It would do a great deal of good. You seem to know much about the evils of drink, but you do not know as much as I know; and I have come to see that this is no business for a Christian man to be engaged in." That merchant did not die in the business.

I talked again and again privately with another merchant about his giving up the business. For a long time I did not think my words were having any effect. One day I met him at an auction, and he brought me to one side and said: "I want to tell you something that will please you." He had such a look of gladness in his eyes I was surprised. But I was more surprised when he told me the cause of his gladness. As if he were throwing off a great weight that had been crushing him down he said with a sigh of relief: "I have got rid of the saloon."

A young man came from a farm and opened a saloon. He married a nice country girl. Neither of them seemed comfortable in the bar. He became suddenly ill, and I was requested to visit him. I visited him several times before his death. I never saw more affection between 'a husband and wife than I witnessed at that death bedside. He told me he did not know what he was doing, else he would never have entered the business, and was no sooner in it than he wished to be out of it, but did not see clearly how to give it up. "At any rate," he said, "my heart was not in it." Seldom in the course of my ministry have I seen greater resignation in the presence of death than I saw in that young man's face. I was astonished to find that some professing Christians refused to attend his funeral because he was a saloon-keeper! I do not say anything about the Christianity of those professors. It may have been only very narrow. It may have been worse. *God's Bar* is for the saloon-man, for them, and for me. We must all appear there. And who can stand when He appeareth on the Great White Throne?

I went one Saturday night to visit a wine-merchant who never came to public worship. He had not been in his family pew for years. I asked him to come to church. He said he could not come. I asked what reason he had for staying away. He became a little annoyed at my persistency. But I was bent on making some inroad to his heart, and at last he said he kept a yard; that many country people stabled their horses with him; that he had several head of cattle to be driven out to grass; and that his time was so much taken up with horses and cattle he had no time for church. I looked at him earnestly and said: *"Supposing you dropped dead behind your counter some Saturday night who would look after the horses and cattle? You'll have to take time to die."* His feeling of annoyance passed away at once. He became gentle as a lamb, while he looked intently into my eyes and said: "I never thought of that before."

THE HAPPY ART OF CATCHING MEN

To my surprise and the surprise of many others, he was in the church twice the next day! He continued to attend twice every Sunday for many months. He was absent one Sunday, but continued his attendance again after a visit of enquiry from me. I preached at a morning service from the text, "What shall it profit a man if he shall gain the whole world and lose his own soul?" That man was in his pew and he never took his eyes off me while I was preaching. When going along the street after the service he said to another member of my congregation: "I believe Mr. Patterson wrote that sermon for me." It so happened that he was much in my thoughts as I was preparing it. I believe it was not preached to him in vain. On the Saturday night I received a message to go down to his house, as *he had dropped dead behind his counter!*

At his funeral a labouring man said to me: "He was a better man than some people thought. He had a kindly heart. I used to buy some groceries and provisions from him, but had not been going to him for some time. He asked me one day as I was passing, why I passed his shop now. I am not a drinker and he knew I was not. He did not want me in for drink. I said that money was hard to get and that sometimes I had none to pay for things I needed. 'Well,' he said, 'don't bother about the paying. The children must get bread. Don't let them want. Come in for a bag of flour whenever you like, and just pay me when it suits yourself.' And," added the labouring man, "that's more than some of the grocers up the town would have said."

I have been at several saloon-keepers' deathbeds, and have heard their dying testimonies to the effect that their hearts were not in the business at all, and that they would have liked to have got out of it if they had seen their way how. After the Catch-my-Pal movement started in Armagh I went to visit a wine

merchant who was dying. He congratulated me on
the success it was having in gathering up the drinkers
and said: *"You have got the stick by the right end
this time."* I know persons now in the trade who
have told me they will get out of it as soon as they
can. One of them told me recently that he considered there could be no true prosperity in such a trade,
that it was *a dirty business from top to bottom, bringing men into contact with all that was filthy in society,
and making them filthier still.* He is setting about de-
veloping a new way of making a livelihood for the
rest of his days.

It may be said that these men should come out of the
business at once if they see it to be an evil thing.
Some of them have done so. Many of them have not
done so. But we must look for a greater manifestation
of self-sacrifice and spiritual *abandon* on the part of
Christians generally before we can expect much
moral heroism from those who are supposed by many
Christians to have no Christianity at all.

While I have told in another chapter what I think
of those saloon-keepers who have tried to bring down
to the gutter again men and women who have taken
the Catch-my-Pal pledge, I desire to state most em-
phatically that I don't put all saloon-keepers in the
same box, and that I consider temperance reformers
who are continually denouncing the saloon-keepers are
on the wrong tack. I have no sympathy whatever
with the business, but I confess I have much sympathy with many of those engaged in it. If I call every
saloon a human slaughter-house I do not call every
saloon-keeper a murderer. I am not prepared to stand
at a saloon door and pass my judgment on the person
behind the bar as a child of the Devil. If I had been
brought up as a saloon-keeper's son, or had been apprenticed to the trade when I really did not know
what I was being apprenticed to, and to-day was standing behind a bar, having conscientious scruples as to

the way I was making my money, I should not like to think that self-righteous people were passing by my door and pointing with the finger of contempt at me while they said: "That is a child of the Devil in there: he is going straight to hell." With my conscientious scruples I might be nearer the Kingdom of God while standing behind the bar than the man with a proud spirit passing my door to a prayer-meeting, for "the proud He knoweth afar off." We do not know what convictions God may be planting in the garden of even a saloon-man's soul. I will therefore try to look at him as through God's eyes while I say:

"The love of God is broader
    Than the measure of man's mind,
And the heart of the Eternal
    Is most wonderfully kind."

If a saloon-keeper has a sincere desire to get out of the business and does not see his way how, *nevertheless he does well to have that desire in his heart.* Let us not break the bruised reed or quench the smoking flax. God in Jesus Christ never overlooks the faintest glimmer of a desire after a better life in the bosom of the worst of His fallen children. That desire is not of the devil's planting.

The man behind the bar of the saloon I leave *before the bar of God.*

I often wonder how Jesus captivated the heart of her out of whom He cast seven devils. He did not flout her sin in her face. This at any rate is sure. Perhaps if some of those engaged in the drink trade were approached in the spirit in which Jesus must have approached the woman, they would be so captivated as to come out of the business and empty their barrels in the gutter into which they formerly sent their customers, and their doing so would be as the pouring out of ointment on the head of Him Who thus, by human means, won them to His service.

148

CHAPTER, XXIX

ATTRACTIONS, COUNTER-ATTRACTIONS AND COUNTER-INFLUENCES

AFTER much experience in the Catch-my-Pal crusade I am more and more convinced that many of the persons who frequent the saloons do so, not so much because they love drink as because they love the fellowship they find in drink. People will club together. The *craving for fellowship* must vent itself. We must not assume that that craving craves for a debauched fellowship. The saloons have been almost the only places where it has been able to gratify itself; and the gratification of fellowship has thus been associated with the gratification of drink.

The saloons are usually most attractive. They are well lighted, gaudily decorated, and so arranged that friends can sit together as long as they please, free from the feeling of being in the way after they have had their drink. The very arrangement of the bottles in the saloons has an attraction for many of those who frequent them. Music and other attractions are being provided more lavishly, and altogether the saloons are being so equipped that men who find but little comfort around their own huddled firesides find it pleasant to sit in the saloon lounge.

If better houses were provided for the toilers of the country there would be less patronage given by them to the saloon. The Christian conscience is beginning to manifest itself in such a manner as to step in to the great manufacturer's office, and to say: *"The time has come when you must give less to public subscrip-*

149

tion lists and give more to the providing of Christian accommodation to those who help you to make your money. They are not 'hands'; they are SOULS; and it must be seen that they have homes in which the soul and the soul's temple shall have a chance."

But while better housing will greatly help in solving the drink problem, and while the true counter-attraction to the saloon is the well-ordered and well-appointed home, *the craving for fellowship must have some public recognition.* If we swoop down upon a town in a well organised attack of Good Samaritanship, and gather up nearly all the drinkers into a total abstinence brotherhood, as has been done in many places, especially in Ireland, in the course of the Catch-my-Pal campaign, we must see that this brotherhood is supplied with the means of gratifying itself along the lines of brotherhood. It is, therefore, absolutely necessary to establish counter-attractions to the saloons.

Unfortunately the counter-attractions usually provided do not attract. In the large cities the rapid development of well appointed refreshment rooms is one of the characteristics of our modern social life. But in the smaller towns and villages we are too familiar with the temperance hotel or coffee shop which savours of oil-cloth, onions and petroleum. The saloon gives the impression that no expense has been spared to make it attractive. The temperance café often gives the impression that every expense has been saved to make it unattractive. The Christian community must provide something better than this if men and women are to be kept out of the saloons.

Temperance saloons should have public bars with all the attractiveness of daintily and artistically arranged bottles. They should be illuminated and decorated in the very best style. There should be reading rooms, recreation rooms, and, if necessary, smoking rooms, and every department should be run in the strictest cleanliness. Into these saloons clergy and churchwardens, ministers and elders, Sabbath school superintendents and teachers, communicants and all professing Christians could go without suspicion.

Respectable and self-respecting men and women will be ashamed to be seen going into the bars while the attractive total abstinence saloon is in the street, for there will no more be heard as an excuse for going into the bar: "Well, you see I have nowhere else to go." No man likes to be considered fond of drink. If the total abstinence saloon is in the street it will be considered that the man who goes into the bar is fond of drink and goes there for IT. Public opinion begins to make itself felt along the footpath.

An attempt has been made to develop counter-attractions under the auspices of the Catch-my-Pal movement in many places in Ireland, and in some places in England and Scotland, but lack of funds prevents it from being carried out to the best advantage. But what has been done has proved, if proof were necessary, that it is by means of the Total Abstinence Saloon or Club that the best results may be procured and secured. And here I may be permitted to give the testimony of Mr. Justice Boyd, in his address to the Grand Jurors of County Antrim at the Assizes in March, 1911. He said: "He could congratulate them on one fact, the large reduction in the number of people who had been convicted of drunkenness in the county. He was glad that that crime, for he called it a crime, was disappearing. Within the last three years the drunkenness returns had shown a decrease of over a thousand cases. Last year about three hundred and seventy-five less cases of drunkenness were reported by the police than in the year before. He was sure they were all considerably indebted to the efforts that had been made by the gentleman who had originated that good Catch-my-Pal movement in the country for the purpose of trying to get people to give up drink, and to keep their neighbours from the evils of drunkenness. They had all reasons to be thankful to that gentleman who had been led to take the course he had done, and who had been so successful in his efforts. Another thing which he thought was a matter of congratulation resulting from that movement was the establishment of working-men's clubs in several places, where reasonable litera-ture and amusements were provided for those who wished to frequent them. They were considerably used, and were found of inestimable advantage in the country. He hoped they would progress still further and that the effect of the movement would be a de-crease of crime, a great quantity of which proceeded from intemperance."

At the Meeting of the General Assembly of the Irish Presbyterian Church in 1911, Dr. Macmillan was able to say in his Annual Temperance Report: "There never was such a full and jubilant note on the subject of counter-attractions. In no less than thirty Presbyterial centres (there are thirty-seven Presby-teries in the Church) are counter-attractions reported as existing. At no time has the subject engaged so much the attention of practical men and women. Read-ing-rooms have come into existence all over the coun-try; and it is pleasant to see numbers of working men —young and old—consulting the papers, engaging in conversation, interested in bagatelle, draughts, or dom-inoes; and such places of rendezvous are to be found not only in important towns, but also in villages and rural districts."

Catch-my-Pal halls are being erected in many cen-tres throughout the country for public and other meet-ings of the Union. These, while affording opportu-nities for the members to associate with one another, are, at the same time, helping to *give permanency to the cause.*

Wherever I have gone on this crusade I have advocated the establishment of counter-attractions, and I am glad to be able to say that not only in Ireland, but also in other countries, Catch-my-Pal reading-rooms and clubs have been instituted in centres so far apart as Bedford, Ventnor, Stratford-on-Avon, Inverness, and Kingston, Jamaica.

Anything which gives a man a healthy interest in matters outside his own narrow groove in life has an uplifting influence which draws him away from the sordid associations of the saloon. Just now there is no institution exercising a greater counter-influence on the drinker than the picture palace. We must not overlook the various ways besides education by which science is helping to solve the drink problem. The kinematograph, the motor car, the telephone, and the typewriter are all at work in solving the problem.

At the *picture palace* the meanest villager can view mankind from China to Peru, and gain as much knowledge of life in other countries in an hour as his father would have been unable to gather in a week from books. He can find cleaner amusement with his eyes on the screen than he can find with his ears at a bar. He can go home to bed from a kinematograph show feeling that there are so many things of interest in the world there is no need for him, a man with a mind, to let his brains be stolen by whisky. He feels better in the morning after he has seen a little of this world on a screen, than in the morning after he has seen two moons at the saloon door. He can bring his wife and children with him to the panopticon, and go home feeling that he has done his part in giving them a happy hour, and he knows how much better it was to have done that than to have spent all his money on himself before going back to send his wife and children to a night in hell. The kinematograph is one of God's instruments for drawing the life blood of the drink trade.

The *motor car* and all kinds of motor vehicles are

helping to solve the problem, for people know that it will not do, in these days of swift traffic, to be dandering about the streets half dazed with drink. In the days of the horse the policeman did not pay so much attention to the man "half seas over" as he does to-day. Traffic cannot wait on the drinker now.

The *telephone* keeps the merchant on the alert in his office. He used to meet his customer and transact his business by personal dealing. He took time over it. He wasted time over it. He drank over it, as the one he was doing business with was in no greater hurry than himself. They could not meet and part again without some good fellowship, and so they had their glass together. But now the telephone intervenes. Personal dealing is almost gone. Business is now business. It will not do for a merchant to be half asleep in his office to-day. A fortune may depend on a telephone call. He must be wide awake. A man was speaking into a telephone one day and could not understand what the person at the other end was saying. He became irritated and said:

"Is a blithering idiot talking into this telephone?"

"Not at this end," was the response. He understood that time! It will not pay to be considered a "blithering idiot" in an up-to-date business house to-day, and the telephone has done more to sharpen men's wits at business, and to keep drink away from business hours, than any other instrument or influence in the commercial world.

The *typewriter* is doing its share. The typist has to be considered. No man will demean himself before his typist by being so much under the influence of drink that he cannot dictate a business letter.

These are some of the influences which are at work in the "waking up" of Uncle Sam. When *aeroplanes* become a commonplace, his eyes will be completely open, and he will see that if he cannot stand in slippery places when drunk much less will he be able, when in that condition, to walk on the wings of the wind

CHAPTER XXX

Touch the Button

For the purpose of giving publicity to the pledges taken in this campaign men and women are expected to wear a button or brooch. As soon as a number of persons have signed the pledge at a public meeting they are all asked to put on the badge of the Union that all who meet them may know what side they are on.

The wearing of the badge has been one of the most potent causes of the success of the movement. The badge has served as an introduction to talk about temperance work with those who might want to avoid such talk. A man with a button in his coat meets another without a button, and says to him: "Have you not 'taken the button' yet?" There is no need to say a word about temperance or signing a pledge. People have found the greatest ease in talking to their friends about "taking the button" when they never would have ventured to speak to them about taking the pledge.

At the close of my address one night in Belfast a large number of persons came to the front to sign their names. I asked them to put on the badges. A personal friend of mine said to me: "Patterson, I'll sign your pledge but I'll not put on your button."

I asked him: "Why?"

He said: "I don't believe in badges and signs."

"Well," I said, "you and I have been friends for some years, and I ask you to put on the button just for one week for friendship's sake."

"All right," he said, "then I will."

I put the button in his coat. On that day week I met him on the street. He ran up to me and said: "Patterson, I believe in the button."

I asked him how he had become converted to his belief.

He said: "I have three friends, and for years I have been watching them getting more and more into drinking habits. I often wished to speak to them on the matter and never had courage to do so. Indeed, I thought they would take my mention of it as an insult. Since I put on the button this day week my three friends have met me in three different places and at different times on the street, and each one of them caught hold of my coat and, pointing to the button, said: 'What is that you have got?' I said: 'That is the Catch-my-Pal button!' You see, they started the conversation, I saw my opportunity and embraced it, and I got the three of them to take the pledge and put on the button. *I believe in the button.*"

The use of the button has fostered the feeling of brotherhood and sisterhood among those who wear it. I have heard many stories of how friendships have been formed in trains and trams by those to whom the button was an introduction. A young minister told me the following story: "I was going along the road one Saturday evening from the railway station to a manse about a mile and a half away. I met a man who said: 'Good-evening, your reverence; you'll let me carry your bag for you.' I thanked him and let him have my bag. We walked and we talked, and several times I asked him to give the bag to me. But he said: 'No, your reverence; I'll carry your bag to the manse for you.' He handed me the bag at the manse gate, and I asked him why he was so kind to me, a stranger. He said: 'Well, your reverence, you see, here's my button. I belong to the button men; and last night I was at the Catch-my-Pal meeting, and the man who addressed us said, 'Men, if any of you see another man who wears the button and think you can do him a good turn, then do it to him as a brother button man.' And, your reverence, when I saw you coming along I said to myself: 'Here's a wee man with a big bag, and he has got the button. I can do him a good turn; I'll carry the bag of a button man.' "

The button on a man's coat acts like an engagement ring on the finger of a girl: *it keeps off the other fellows!* Behind the button there is a feeling of security. While I believe in the depravity of human nature I do not believe there are many men in any neighbourhood who will deliberately try to tamper with the total abstinence virtue that the button stands for on the bosom of a brother.

But saloon-keepers of the meaner type have tried to tamper with that virtue by all kinds of dodgery. They issued, in some cases, to their customers at the bar, buttons almost like the Catch-my-Pal buttons. Passersby would not know the difference between the two buttons, and would naturally say: "There are your Catch-my-Pal men! You see them going into and out of the saloons every day. What is the use of joining a society like that?" Free drinks and free suppers have been offered by saloon-keepers to members of the Union to induce them to break their pledges. Members have gone into saloons to get mineral waters, and have found that the *bar men put whisky or some other intoxicant into the drink on the sly.* In this way men who were formerly hard drinkers have been taken unawares, and have fallen into their old habits. Bar men have been known to offer a quart of their best whisky to men for their buttons, and to exhibit buttons thus procured in their windows, with a view to bringing the movement into disgrace.

We have often heard it said by those in the trade that they never invite anyone in to drink. They need

157

never open their mouths to talk like this again after the mean tricks and devilish dodgery many of them have resorted to in connection with this crusade.

If the saloon-keepers have tried to play tricks on the pals, it is interesting to learn how they themselves have been tricked. For instance, a drinker who had not joined the Union found a button on the street. He put it in his coat and loitered at the door of a saloon. The bar-man saw him and his button, and, thinking he was a member of the Union, offered him a drink for his button. The man at once consented, and the bar-man thought he had won back a customer. What was his chagrin when the drinker told him he had found the button on the street, and that there was no reason to crow over a fallen pal! Drinkers have procured buttons in many ways, and used them for procuring whisky under false pretences.

It is pleasant to be able to record cases of great moral heroism on the part of heavy drinkers in resisting the saloon-keepers' temptations.

*   *   *   *   *   *   *

A man who was perhaps the most notorious drinker in his town was asked in by a saloon-keeper to the bar. The saloon-keeper offered him a quart of whisky for his button. He took the bottle of whisky and handed the saloon-keeper the button. He went to the bar door and smashed the bottle on the pavement, and went back to the saloon-keeper and said: "There is your whisky outside. I can get another button for tuppence."

*   *   *   *   *   *   *

A man well known to me as an almost abandoned drinker told me his experience of temptation in a saloon: One day I went into a pub to get a bottle of lemonade. The publican said to me:

"Will you drown your button, John?" (A man was said to drown his button when he gave it in exchange for a glass of whisky.)

158

"What will you give me to drown it in?" said I.

"I'll give you a glass of the best whisky in the house," said he.

"Done!" said I. "Put down your whisky."

He put down the glass of whisky on the counter, and I put down my button beside it. He was going to take the button for the glass, but I said:

"Drown that button."

"What do you mean?" said he.

"I mean that *you* are to drown that button," said I.

"I don't know what you mean," said he.

"I mean that you are to put that button into the whisky and drown it," said I.

He put the button into the whisky.

"Now," said I: "Take the button out of the whisky with your sugar tongs."

He took the button out, and, your reverence, there was not a drop of whisky on the button! I held it up before him and said:

"Look here, my man, there's not a drop of whisky on the button."

I then put the button in my coat again and patted it as, looking over the counter, I said to the publican:

"There's not a drop of whisky on it. That button is whisky-proof. And if the button is whisky-proof, *the man that wears the button is whisky-proof;* no more of your whisky for me."

This man has not tasted strong drink for over four years.

* * * * * * *

"What is that you have got in your coat?" said a bar-man to one of his former customers standing opposite his shop.

"That's the Catch-my-Pal button," said the pal. "And what is that you have got up there?" he added, pointing to the saloon signboard.

"Oh, that's my sign that I am licensed to sell drink," answered the saloon-keeper.

"Well," said the other, "if that's your sign that you are licensed to sell drink, *this is my sign that I am licensed not to drink your drink.*"

* * * * * * *

One day at a seaside resort I saw a jarvey sitting on his jaunting car. His horse was restive and, as I passed by, I said: "I think that horse would need the button."

"Well, yer rivirince, if the horse has not tuk the button, he knows that the man behind the horse has tuk it."

I then saw that the jarvey was a "button man." He told me how he had been a big drinker, how he had joined the Union in his town, and how the horse knew the difference in the treatment it received 'from him now as compared with what it used to receive before he took the button.

* * * * * * *

The present Dean of St. Patrick's, Dublin, was formerly Dean of Clogher. In a recent letter to me he wrote: "On July 12th, there were thousands of Orangemen in Enniskillen, and not a tipsy man among them. It was noted that from under nearly every sash there peeped out your little button."

* * * * * * *

JOHNNIE: "Now, do you think I look like a man that would barter my freedom for a button?"

JIMMIE: "I think you look like one that does not know the meaning of freedom. It would need more than a poor little button to break your chain."

JOHNNIE: "Man, it would."

JIMMIE: "You admit that?"

JOHNNIE: "Certainly."

JIMMIE: "Where is your freedom, then?"

SAMMIE: "Come away, Johnnie, he's one too many for you."

JOHNNIE: "Och! away *you;* the man's right!"

TOUCH THE BUTTON

In many districts in Ulster, and, I suppose, in most places, it used to be considered a cowardly thing for a man to take the pledge. The public use of the button has almost entirely changed the common opinion about pledge-taking. Instead of being now considered a coward if he takes the pledge, *a man is considered a coward if he does not take it.*

A man used to come for a pledge in the way he came for a license of marriage. I was one of the licensers of marriage in the Presbytery of Armagh, and in that capacity I had some curious experiences with men at that interesting juncture in their lives.

The candidate for license would stand at the door for some time wondering if he should knock. When, at last, he made up his mind to knock, he did it so gently that the maid did not hear him. He began to think the passers-by were taking rather too much interest in him, so he ventured to give one big knock in the middle of a number of "wee" ones.

When the maid came to the door he appeared like one suffering from creeping paralysis as he nervously asked: "Is his reverence in?"

He was invited into the hall. He leaned against the door while the maid told the minister. His reverence came out and enquired: "What can I do for you, sir?"

Seeing the peculiar look on the face that indicated dread of a licensing ordeal the minister asked the poor victim into his study. There the candidate sat for about thirty-five minutes talking to the minister about all sorts of things but the thing in hand. Crops, coal, weather, politics, etc., were all passed in review. It was part of the minister's pleasure to see the candidate writhing with desire to make known his errand, but deliberately to refuse to help him out of his hole. At last, when he thought he could keep his secret no longer, the victim of a matrimonial propensity ventured to rub his palms together and to count his fingers, and to look out from under his brows at the minister while he said: "Your reverence, I say, your reverence, I was—I .was—I was thinkin' of changin' my mode of life, your reverence."

The blue papers were then produced by the minister. All the necessary forms were signed and witnessed. The precious license was put away in the inside pocket of the vest near the heart. Good-night was said, and the happy man walked out into the street. He went fairly steadily till he heard a footfall just behind him. He started like a guilty thing upon a fearful summons. ·He thought he had been tracked and that all was known! He felt as if everyone he met had X-rays in his eyes and saw through his two coats and waist-coat to the little blue paper. He walked as if to a scaffold till he reached the door of his beloved. He did not mince matters with the knocker there. He was soon in the angelic presence.

He was a great man then! He would go through fire and water then! He did not talk about the price of coal then! He looked at her most endearingly, and she looked at him most expectantly. He put his hand over his heart, and, rubbing his bosom, he said: "Ach, an' sure it's just there, my darlin'."

And if she had only known what a shape he had made before the minister's maid, and what a waste of the minister's time had been caused by his sheer cowardice, she would have said: "Take yourself and your wee blue paper out of this. It's A MAN I want!"

Many men have come to me after this fashion for pledges in former days. But in connection with this campaign they seem to have no hesitancy in letting all the world know what side they are on. And nothing has more helped to change the attitude of men and women towards pledge-taking than the public wearing of the button.

CHAPTER XXXI

"THREE KINDS OF FLY"

IN *all our attempts at catching men we should study the man to be caught. Lack of method and unmitigated fussiness are characteristic of too much Christian work.*

One day a lady came to ask me to go and speak to a friend of hers about his drinking habits. I said I could not see my way to go near him, and I asked her why she came to me. "Well," she said, "you have been so successful in saving men from drink, I thought that you would surely be the one to see this man." I told her I could not go to him, and when she asked me why I could not go I said, "If you want to send your friend to the devil altogether you will send me in on him."

"Why, what in all the world do you mean?" said she.

"I mean just this,—*that man is not my pal.* I do not know him. He does not know me. I never heard of him before. If I went to see him I should have to break the ice and gradually let him know that I had come to talk to him about his drinking habits. He would then begin to rage in his bosom, and all the venom and wrath and spleen of his nature would manifest themselves in his face, and he would storm at me and say, 'What do you mean by coming here? Who has been going behind my back to tell you, a stranger, about my drinking habits? What right have you, a stranger, to intrude upon the privacy of my life? Take yourself and your good advice through that door!'

And he would almost pitch me out, and down his office steps. Certainly I'll not go near him. That would not be 'Catch-my-Pal.' But do you know three of that man's acquaintances, who know that he drinks? And he knows that they know? Will you go and get three such friends, pals of his, in fact, to band themselves into a little brotherhood of salvation for saving that man? If you will do this you will be doing a much wiser thing than if you ask me to go to him, and you will be all the more likely to accomplish your friend's deliverance from drink." She said she thought it would be wiser, and that she would go and do as I suggested.

In vain is the net spread in the sight of any bird. It will not do for me to buttonhole every drinker that I know. I may know that a man is a drinker while I *do not know the man.* Unless I know the man, it may prove very foolish if I attempt to save him from his drinking. It would be more wise if I tried to get one who really knows him to become interested in him and to attempt to make the rescue.

As I was going along an Irish road one day with a medical student who was on his way to fish in a river, he said to me, "There is a peculiar little fish in that river. *I have to put three kinds of fly on my line at three different times of the day to catch that one kind of fish."* And I thought, "What a lesson from this fisher of fish for me a fisher of men!" What was the lesson? If that young student, in addition to his other studies, went to the trouble of studying that little fish, which is seemingly worthless except for the fun of catching it, to such an extent that he knows exactly what kind of fly he must put on his line, at three different times of the day, to land it on the bank, why should not I, a fisher of men, go to the trouble of studying the man I want to catch?" And so I lay stress on the thought at the back of the name Catch-*my*-Pal. Every one of us knows some person who is either down or going down, some one whom we can call friend, chum, pal,—one who is so intimate that we have every opportunity of looking into the nooks and crannies of his or her life, and to make a close study of the particular influence we should bring to bear upon his or her life so as to effect a rescue. The bait used at one time may be quite out of place at another; so we have to study times, and seasons, and all kinds of idiosyncrasies, that we may at last decide on the *proper bait,* and the *proper time,* and the *proper method* of approach, to land our pal on the bank of a pure and sober life. Let us have a very homely illustration. A young man goes in search of a wife. He goes a "courting." The very word implies caution, patience, insight, foresight, the wiles of wisdom, the determination to succeed, the study of his object, the carefulness that avoids mistakes, the gentleness that draws, the weaving of webs, the choosing of bait, the throwing of the line, the jumping, the biting, the catching, and the landing! And when the landing is accomplished he feels rewarded for all the trouble of the courting. Indeed, he could wish that it had all to be done again, for the joy of a second landing. And if I am to be a successful fisher of men, landing them on the bank of the river of life, I must court my pals. *In the social world you court your "gal" and catch her. And in the social reform world I court my pal and catch him.* In courting one has to use many a "fly." Sometimes more than three kinds of fly are necessary in the course of one day to attract and gain attention. And if I am to CATCH MY PAL it may be necessary to use many kinds of fly before I can meet with success. I cannot possibly know what kind of fly I should use to attract and catch a man whom I do not know. But if I attempt to catch a PAL, I can study my pal so that, by all the loving wiliness of personal knowledge, I may land him at the feet of Jesus. Sometimes by a wise word, sometimes by a loving look, sometimes by a winning smile, sometimes by a friendly hand-grasp, sometimes by a stern rebuke, sometimes by an appeal to manly quality, sometimes by a Christian suggestion, sometimes by a business suggestion, and sometimes by a prayer when every other art proves a failure, may a man be won, a pal be caught, a new recruit gained for the forces of God and Righteousness.

If a fisher of fish studies his fish, the fisher of men must study his man. To study a man aright he must study the Son of Man who knows what is in man. And He says, "Follow Me and I will make you to become fishers of men." The art of Christian Fishing is the most delightful and happy of all the fishing arts. But it is usually overlooked that it IS an art. And artless fishing for men is, perhaps, *the most conspicuous weakness of the Church of Christ to-day*. If the world is to be won for God and Purity the Church must see that she turns out "Complete Anglers" to go a-fishing. *Every Christian Congregation should be a Training School of Anglers*. Every Christian Congregation should be a Catch-my-Pal Society, in which every person desirous of doing work for the Kingdom of God should be trained in the best methods of work so as to secure the winning of all those within the circuit of that congregation that are in need of winning. The Church has laid great stress on preaching, and rightly so. She has laid great stress on teaching also, and rightly so. *But she has not laid much stress on training; and there she has failed*. All over our civilized world there are great technical schools in which pupils are trained to put in practice the teaching they have received. And we all know what a difference there is between teaching and training. A man may know all about the details of an internal combustion engine and pneumatic tyres and electric arc lamps, but have no experience in the driving of an automobile. Training is the putting of teaching into proper practice. And while the churches

166

have preached and taught, they must, if they are to hold their own, merely as business concerns, to say nothing of them as spiritual concerns, begin to train their members in the happy art of catching men. There is an unlimited field of operations among the young men and the young women of the churches. And what multitudes of Communicants go to the Table of the Lord to profess their loyalty to Him, and go away from the table as *an unorganised crowd,* with no definite aim or object before them as members of a great brotherhood and sisterhood of salvation! As a great motor factory is so organised that every man is specially trained to do a specific work in turning out *a complete machine,* so each congregation should be organised that each member will have a specific work to do for turning out *a purified society.* And when each Christian comes to see it to be his or her duty and privilege and pleasure to work for the catching of at least one other for God, and that other one his or her own PAL, there will be nothing impossible in the wonder-working power of the Church among the ruins of humanity.

When in Salt Lake City I was surprised to hear that every young man and every young woman of the Mormon faith promises to give at least two years of his or her life to the propagation of Mormonism wherever the church wishes to send them. And, certainly, there are no members of any church better trained in the art of catching men than the Mormons. Perhaps it would be nearer the mark if I said "the art of catching women." At any rate the Mormons are trained to be "fishers of men." It is no wonder the Mormon faith is spreading at such a rate as to be the greatest menace to the United States. The success of Mormonism is the result, not so much of preaching or of teaching as it is of training. The late Dr. A. B. Bruce has given us a great book on "The Training of the Twelve." Jesus "made them to become fishers

·of men." And *the greatest work the Church of Jesus Christ has to do to-day is to train her members to be fishers and not bunglers.* Christians must be *wise* as serpents and harmless as doves in their work as fellow-workers with Jesus Christ. He that is *wise* winneth souls. The last words my dear father said to me were, "They that be *wise* shall shine as the brightness of the firmament, and they that turn many to righteousness as the stars for ever and ever."

In all our theological colleges we have Chairs of Pastoral Theology for the purpose of training candidates for the ministry in the art of catching men. In every Christian Congregation there should be such a Chair for the training of young Christians in the art of being fellow-workers together with Jesus Christ. Jesus knew how to adapt Himself to every situation in which He found Himself, and there is nothing in the Gospels so interesting to me, except His death, as *the way He dealt with individuals.* Truly He was the Son of Man and knew what was in man, and knew how to meet every emergency in the way of dealing with every kind of individual that met Him along His way of ministry. Read the first two chapters of St. Mark. You feel as if you were in an American hustle all the time. What impresses you when you thoughtfully read those chapters and lay down your Bible? Why, you say, Jesus was master of every situation; He was ready for every emergency. Surely here is the Wisdom of God incarnate. Surely here is THE ONE Who can train men how to deal with men. We will sit at His feet and hear His word, and we will follow Him that He may train us to be fishers of men. Every Christian Congregation should aim at being a Christian Technical School for training Christian fishers to go out in all wisdom to catch men and save for purity the neighbourhood in which the Congregation is placed.

All this will mean trouble. It will mean an upsetting

of many old methods. It will mean a complete up-heaval in the common ideas regarding congregational life and aims. It will mean an entire reorganisation of most congregational societies. It will introduce the missionary ideal into all departments of Church life. *It will knock the bottom out of the self-complacency with which some congregations contemplate great collections and successful funds, while men and women and children are left outside the church unsought and unsaved.*

How much is a man better than a fish! How necessary that every Christian worker should study the art of "Three Kinds of Fly."

CHAPTER XXXII

THE POINT OF CONTACT

GOD has as many ways of saving men as He has of making men. Never in all the history of the world were two men made alike. No two men in all the world think alike, or speak alike, or write alike, or walk alike, or sin alike. And no two men are saved alike. We cannot tell how many lines may be drawn to the centre of a circle, and we cannot tell how many ways God has of drawing men to Himself. Every tree in the forest casts its own shadow as every tree stands in its own relation to the sun. Each man stands on his own line of relation to God, and he must go along that line, and no other, if he is ever to come to God. But each man's line leads him to the Cross on the way to the Father.

All attempts to save a man from any sin should be made at what is called *the point of contact*. Many of the attempts at saving men fail, because those who make them fail to see that God has no cast-iron way of saving men. One would think, on hearing some preachers, that all men must have quite similar experiences of conversion. But a man's experience of conversion altogether depends on the nature of the sin from which he is converted. And as sin is as varied in its aspects as is the human face, we must not put down any cast-iron rule and say that unless a man is saved according to *that* rule he is not saved at all.

The commonest assumption regarding our attempts at saving men is that we must BEGIN WITH THE SOUL. As far as I know there is no place in the

Bible where we are told that a man's salvation must begin in his soul. And I do not think that we are warranted by any interpretation of Scripture experience in assuming that we must begin the work of salvation with the soul. *God wants to save the MAN. And the soul is not the man.*

I have never seen a ghost. I have never seen a man or a woman without a body. It requires both *a body and a soul* to make a man or a woman. But so much value is attached to the soul by many who are seeking the salvation of their fellows, they almost, if not entirely, overlook the value of the body. Or, if they think of it at all, they consider the body more *an obstacle* to salvation than *an object* of salvation. It is, in their estimation, so much clay, so much dust of the earth. Their attitude to the body might thus be illustrated:—

A lunatic was at large one day. I knew him well. In his lucid intervals he was quite an ordinary person; but when he went off his head he became a tremendous theologian! On this day he overtook a great ecclesiastical dignitary and, eyeing him several times from head to foot, he exclaimed, "Who made you? I say, who made you?" The Ecclesiastic said, "Oh, God made me." "And a great big lump of dirt he did make!" answered the lunatic. Is it not so that, in the eyes of many who are working for the salvation of men, the body is looked upon as not much better than what that lunatic called it?

Now, what is the Scriptural view of the human body? It is the workmanship of God. Listen to the author of that "God-intoxicated" psalm, the 139th. "Thou hast covered me (margin, "knit me together") in my mother's womb. I will praise Thee, for I am fearfully and wonderfully made: marvellous are Thy works; and that my soul knoweth right well. My frame was not hidden from Thee, when I was made in secret, and curiously wrought in the lowest parts of the earth. Thine eyes did see mine unperfect substance, and in Thy book were all my members written, which day by day were fashioned, when as yet there was none of them."

Our bodies are "the temples of the Holy Spirit." We are to "glorify God in our bodies and in our spirits which are His." We are "to present our bodies living sacrifices, holy and acceptable, to God. This is our reasonable service." Paul prays, "May your whole spirit and soul and body be preserved without break or blame till the arrival of our Lord Jesus Christ." Jesus, the Saviour, "will transform this body of our low estate till it resembles the body of His Glory." In the face of such declarations as these, must we not think of the body as very precious in the sight of God, and that He wants to save the body as well as the soul? He does not want to save the soul alone or the body alone, but both soul and body. He must save both if the individual is to be saved, for it requires both to make the individual.

I venture to say that it was not necessary for Jesus to have gone to the grave to save our souls. He saved our souls *before* He gave up the spirit and entered into the state of the dead. In other words, Jesus went into hell before He went into the grave. We might say that *Jesus died twice upon the Cross.* He first died in His soul, and then in His body. He became a lost soul. "He Who knew no sin was made to BE SIN." When He was SIN He was God-forsaken. God-forsakenness is Hell. He could go no further from the Father morally or spiritually than when He became Sin. He then "poured out His soul *unto death*," and we are to "make His soul an offering for our sins." If Jesus thought as little of the human body as some preachers do He never would have gone to the grave, because He wrought out the salvation of our souls when He was crying out, "My God, my God, Why hast Thou forsaken me?" But He wanted to save our bodies too,

and "He bowed His head and gave up His spirit."
He gave up the spirit of His bodily life that He might
become a dead body and enter into the grave from
which, by the power of His resurrection, He might
come forth with the salvation of the body too. *He
saved our souls by the death of His soul, and He
saved our bodies by the death of His body. He poured
out his soul unto death that our souls might live and He
poured out His body unto death that our bodies might
live.* He wanted to save the whole man. And His
fellow-workers must aim at the salvation of the whole
man, body and soul. And it does not matter whether
a man's salvation begins in the body or in the soul as
long as it begins at all. *Sometimes the soul is saved
through the body, and sometimes the body is saved
through the soul.* Jesus Himself used both methods
in the New Testament time, just as both methods were
used in Old Testament time. Naaman's wife had a
little Hebrew maid who told her mistress of the wonderful man, Elisha, the prophet of Jehovah. She said
to her mistress, "Would God my master were with
the prophet that is in Samaria, for then would he re-
cover him of his leprosy." Naaman came to Elisha. I
am sure Elisha could have desired nothing more than
that Naaman should believe in *his* God. But he saw
that the immediate need of Naaman was the cure of
the leprosy, so he told him to go and wash himself in
Jordan. Naaman expected Elisha to mention the name
of his God in working the cure. But the prophet never
mentioned God's name. He simply told Naaman to
go and wash himself. Naaman went and washed, and
his leprosy left him, "and his flesh came again like
unto the flesh of a little child, and he was clean."
This seems like *the Old Testament way of saying that
Naaman was "born again."* He became like a "little
child" as far as his body was concerned. And what
happened then? Why, he immediately made a con-
fession with his soul, as he stood before the man of

173

God and said, "Behold, now I know that there is no
God in all the earth but in Israel." His soul was
reached through the body. Even though he did go
back and bow down in the house of Rimmon he prayed
that the only God would pardon him. He might bow
down in the house of Rimmon as a matter of form,
but his heart would not bow there with his knees.
He went back a believer. He became a believer by
the salvation of his body.

In the New Testament we find Jesus and the Apostles adopting the same method as Elisha in the case of
diseased persons. They wanted these persons to come
to a saving knowledge. And it was usually through
the body the saving knowledge came. In the case of
the sick of the palsy Jesus was beginning the man's
salvation through the soul when He said, "Thy sins
be forgiven thee." But when He was criticised by the
professional theologians as to His method He then
began at the body. It was all the same to Him whether
He said, "Thy sins be forgiven thee," or "Rise, take
up thy bed and walk." It was a matter of indifference
to Jesus whether He began with the soul or with the
body. One was as precious in His sight as the other,
and He was willing to begin with either as long as
the MAN was saved. The usual method with Jesus
was to begin with the body. *He began at the blind
man's eyes. He began at the dumb man's tongue. He
began at the deaf man's ears. He began at the lame
man's feet. He began at the hand of the man whose
hand was withered.* Then, having made a beginning,
*He worked from the HAND to the soul; He worked
from the FEET to the soul; He worked from the
EARS to the soul; He worked from the TONGUE to
the soul; He worked from the EYES to the soul.* And,
when, in the Name of Jesus, we try to bring about a
man's salvation, we must begin at the place where the
man needs salvation most, the most obvious point, the

174

point of contact, the point where the man best understands.

The most obvious salvation that a drunkard needs is salvation from drink. We might take his throat as his diseased part. Let us begin at the diseased part. *Let us begin at the THROAT,* and WORK FROM THE THROAT TO THE SOUL. In other words, let us get the drinker to take a pledge to give up the drink, and then he will be all the more likely to think seriously about life and God.

We send medical missionaries to heathen lands. Why? Is it that we may save their souls? Yes. But is that all we want? If so, then why send medical missionaries? But we want to save MEN and WOMEN and CHILDREN, body and soul. And a medical missionary is more likely to be effective than a non-medical one. Why? Because the heathen mind can understand a bodily cure when it cannot comprehend a spiritual one. If I may be permitted so to use the words: "That is not first which is spiritual, but that which is natural; and afterward that which is spiritual." Through the saved body the Christian medical missionary makes *a highway of sympathy for the King to enter the City of Mansoul.*

In the mission to the drunkards we are dealing with a particular form of disease which is bodily. We therefore attempt the salvation of the body first, in the hope that we may reach the whole MAN, body and soul. We do not say that we are successful in every case. "Were there not ten cleansed? But where are the nine?" But if wisdom is justified of her children, and if a movement is known by its fruits, we have enough evidence of saved LIVES all over the land to make us persuaded that the movement has been of God and has been a wise one in turning many to righteousness.

There are many who stand aloof from and criticise the Catch-my-Pal movement because it does not always, in the first instance, seek the salvation of a man's soul. They say: "If a man is converted he is all right." Yes! But what, exactly, is conversion, and when does a man begin to be converted?

They say: "If a man is born again, he is all right." Yes! But what, exactly, is it to be "born again," and when does a man begin to be born again?

They say: "If the Grace of God could only get a hold of these men and women who have signed the pledge." Yes! But what is the Grace of God? What is it like? How does it manifest itself? Who will undertake to say when the Grace of God begins to lay hold on any of us? There are some who think the Grace of God is a spiritual power which manifests itself in some indefinable way in a man's soul. It may be this, and often is this. But the Grace of God may take the form of public opinion in a man's street.

There are men and women all around us who, if we began to talk to them about their souls, would simply turn away from us. Their spirituality is so low that they hardly understand spiritual conversation. They will not listen to sermons about conversion. They cannot be saved by a direct appeal to the soul. The point of contact at which salvation can be brought to them is not in the soul; it will probably be found in the diseased body craving for drink, or in the bosom of a broken-hearted wife, or in the misery of a half-starved child, or in the squalor of the fireside. If we talk to a drunkard about these things he will understand. If he comes to see that the public opinion in his street is so changed that it will not tolerate these things, but looks on them with loathing and disgust, he will begin to become sensitive to his surroundings; he will feel miserable in running the gauntlet of his street's contempt; his thoughts begin to take a higher level, and his body begins to follow his thought; and if he has no heavenly wisdom to understand what we call heavenly things, he has enough worldly wisdom to understand the worldly thing of his own street's opinion about him.

All our attempts to save a man should be made at the point where he understands. If he cannot bear talk about his soul he can bear talk about his body, and the state into which he has brought his wife and children by his life of debauchery. Once we have got a man to see he is a fool as far as this world is concerned, we have led him very near to the point of wisdom as far as the next world is concerned. If we find that we cannot begin a man's conversion in his soul, let us begin with the body. If we cannot begin at his head, let us begin at his feet. In the Name of Jesus let us begin somewhere. It does not really matter where we begin so long as we begin somewhere. And, if we can make no impression on the man by appealing to his selfish common-sense regarding his own body, let us appeal to him along the line of unselfish common-sense regarding his wife or children, or mother, as the case may be. When we have gained an inch along any one of these lines, let us try with all our hearts to gain another inch, and another, and another, until we have reached the very centre of the citadel of the man's life. Once we have made the least breach in the wall of a man's depraved self it is for us to follow up our endeavour till the whole man is captured for God and purity, as every inch gained by the Japs at Port Arthur was held till they gained the last one. Inch by inch the fortress was taken. The fortress of Mansoul is more baffling than Port Arthur. And, when a man's soul is at last captured for God, who will say when and where the Grace of God began to operate?

Let me give a few instances of how men's souls were saved through the saving of their bodies.

A man came to see me one day and told me his story. "I was a drunkard for *twenty-seven years.* My wife's heart was broken by my bad conduct. My children ran from me in fear when I came home from my work. My home was miserable, and I was in debt. I signed the pledge at a meeting four years ago. Since then I have not tasted drink. I have a new home. I just wish you saw it. My wife is as happy as the day is long. My children now welcome me home. I have family worship every night, and I go to church every Sunday. I have been converted and I am now a communicant. I thank God that He saved me through Catch-my-Pal." When did that man's conversion begin? He is a leading Christian worker in his church to-day.

I know a man in a very good position who almost destroyed his family by his drunken life. He was considered the very worst drinker in his district; and no one thought he could ever give up his craving. He joined the movement as soon as it came to his village. He kept the pledge faithfully, to the surprise of everyone who knew him, and especially to the surprise of his wife and children. He told me he had been a drinker for over forty years. For several months after he signed the pledge he would neither go to his market town nor to Belfast, lest he might be tempted to break it. He prayed for strength to keep it. When he felt strong enough to resist temptation he ventured to go away from home. He went to fairs and markets. He has never taken any drink since he took the pledge over four years ago, though he has come through a time of great physical suffering when he felt the temptation very strong. He has become a communicant and, that he is living a consistent life, all who know him testify. I was conducting a service in a church near his home one Sunday afternoon. He was present. I was told that his wife, who was also present, wished to see me at their house after the service. I suspected why she wished to see me. I saw her and her husband and their children. They were all so happy-looking that I could hardly believe they had ever been looking any other way. *The gratitude I saw in that good woman's eyes that day I shall never forget. I believe she asked me to her house that I might see it. It was worth going round the world to see.* I felt that the Catch-my-Pal movement was justified by the look on that one face. The Salvation of Christ had come to that house.

On New Year's Eve, 1911, I was going into a large hall in Belfast to conduct a Watch-night service. Two labouring men whom I did not know accosted me at the door. One said: "Your reverence, I want to tell you how glad I am to see you."

"Why are you glad to see me?" I asked.

"I want to tell you that your button has been the means of my salvation."

On expressing my delight to hear such news I asked him how it came about.

He said: "I 'took the button' two years ago. I was a great drinker. But I have never tasted a drop for two years. I went into a Gospel meeting three weeks ago, and I gave myself to Christ that night. I never would have been in that meeting at all if I had not 'taken the button.' I have been wearing this button for two years, and it has been the means of my salvation; but I did not know it till three weeks ago."

His companion added, "And I can say the same as my pal, your reverence, for I 'took the button' at the same time, and I was converted at the same meeting three weeks ago."

The Gospels record the gratitude of at least one woman out of whom Jesus cast seven devils. The Catch-my-Pal movement can point to many women who were considered as quite abandoned to drink and to all ungodliness, but who are to-day living pure Christian lives. And the gratitude I have seen in *their* eyes testifies to the presence of Jesus in their hearts.

179

"I've found a Friend; O such a Friend!
   He loved me ere I knew Him;
He drew me with the cords of love,
   And thus He bound me to Him;
And round my heart still closely twine
   Those ties which nought can sever,
For I am His and He is mine
   For ever and for ever."

I have always laid great stress on the fact that total
abstinence is not enough to save a man. I have often
found persons who seemed to think that total abstinence was a summing up of all the virtues. *They
suffer from a surfeit of self-satisfaction if not from a
surfeit of spirits.* But a man may be a total abstainer
and be a blackguard. He may be a total abstainer and
be a liar. He may be a total abstainer and be a Sab-
bath-breaker. He may be a total abstainer and be on
the way to hell. But while total abstinence is not
enough, it may prove to be the first step for some men
on the way to heaven. It may be the first showing
of the crucifying of the flesh which is only complete
when we are filled with the Spirit of the Crucified One.
If a man who has been a great drinker gives up his
drinking, he may not be converted, but he is in the way
of being converted; if he is not saved, he is in the way
of being saved. *He is more likely to believe to the
saving of his soul at a sober fireside than he was at a
drunken one.* And the Lord is adding to the church
daily such as are being thus saved by the hand of the
Catch-my-Pal movement. This is the testimony
borne by ministers and other Christian workers in all
districts where the movement has had a chance, and
it is the testimony I am continually receiving from men
and women whom I meet as I go about from place
to place.

CHAPTER XXXIII

A GREATER WATERLOO

WHEN we go to war we try to throttle our enemy, lest our enemy throttle us. We have been hearing long enough that if the State does not throttle the drink traffic, the drink traffic will throttle the State. We have heard from the Lord Chief Justice of England that, in his opinion, formed after many years at the bar and on the bench, about ninety-five *per cent.* of the crime of that country is due to drink. We have heard that Mr. Gladstone used to say that drink was responsible for more deaths and disasters than all the horrors of war, pestilence, and famine. We have heard from the Lord Chancellor of England that if we could solve the drink problem we could, at the same time, solve about seventy *per cent.* of the other social problems that are facing us to-day. There is not one of us who does not know the truth of these things we have so often heard. If we are persuaded of the truth of these statements it is surely time that each of us began to think seriously whether the conditions which make these statements possible are to continue to remain at our doors. If they are so to continue we must admit that we, as a country, are in the grip of our enemy. We are not in a state of siege. The siege is over, and the enemy is in the streets. The drink king is ruling over us with an unmerciful hand. He has been chastising us with scorpions. He has brought hell into our homes and turned our people into *his garden of delight, the city slum.*

There is hardly a home in our land from which no

member of the family has gone to do battle with the drink. There is hardly a home in our land in which one beloved one has not lain dead at the hand of this enemy. The destroyer has come over every threshold. And as we would shut and barricade our doors to keep an armed man from entering to slay us, so we need to rouse the people to a true sense of their danger in the presence of this foe of the family life.

This is a question that concerns every fireside. Our aim as Social Reformers must be to get the people to arise and shut the doors not only of their homes, but of their country against this foe. This is a question for the people. *It is first and foremost and preeminently a question for the people.* But the people think it is a question for ministers of religion and church officers generally. They say: "Let the ministers fight this battle for us." But the ministers never can do it. The people say: "Let the church-wardens and elders, and class leaders, and Sabbath School teachers, and superintendents fight the battle for us." But these can never do it. The people say: "Let the leaders of Social Reform fight this battle for us." But these can never do it. Why? Simply because no officer ever yet won a battle. The officer gives the lead, and, woe to the officer who, in the day of battle, will not give the lead; *but when the lead is given, it is for the rank and file to see the thing through.* Will you who read this little book join with me in the rank and file, and rise and do *your* duty?

I had the pleasure of addressing a thousand boys at the Naval School at Greenwich, all sons of the British Navy, and all preparing to enter the Navy. At the close of my address I asked the boys to strike out for a TEMPERANCE TRAFALGAR. I said: "Boys! Who won the Battle of Trafalgar?" A thousand boys yelled: "Nelson!" I answered with a loud and vehement "NO!" The boys stared at me and at one another in blank amazement. They were quite silent while their eyes wandered about, and it seemed as if they were all asking one another: "What does the man mean? He says *it wasn't Nelson who won the Battle of Trafalgar!* Didn't *you* always hear it was Nelson? And didn't *you,* and *you,* and *you?* What on earth does that wild Irishman mean by saying it wasn't? He does not know one word of English history. What does he mean?"

I said: "I know what you are thinking and saying; and, boys, you are quite right, you are quite right. It was Nelson's genius that planned the battle, and his genius that composed the immortal signal, 'ENGLAND EXPECTS THAT EVERY MAN WILL DO HIS DUTY.' Nelson was pierced by a French bullet and fell, and was able to command no longer. But the battle went on. Why? Because the inspiration of that signal got into the men, and the men jumped up into the inspiration of the signal; and, boys, it was your grandsires, your grandfathers and great grandfathers, the rank and the file, every man on every ship on that immortal day who did his duty, and *saw Trafalgar through.*" When the boys saw my point, that the fight was fought and the victory won *by their own grandsires,* they shouted and cheered approval in such a fashion as to fill any Britisher's heart with pride. I asked them all to strike out for a Greater Trafalgar, to be won by us over a greater foe than ever the French were. They all rose at my request, and when I said: "Now, boys, for a Temperance Trafalgar!" they held up their hands and repeated a Total Abstinence pledge, and with clenched fists above their heads all those thousand boys said word by word after me:

"WE—WILL—SEE—THIS—THING— THROUGH!"

In this Greater Trafalgar America's God expects every man will do his duty, and every woman too.

THE HAPPY ART. OF CATCHING MEN

In the thick of the fight at Waterloo, Wellington saw the Ninety-Fifth Regiment wavering before the superior power of the French. He rode up and shouted: "Stand firm, Ninety-Fifth! We must not be beaten! What would they say in England?" The Ninety-Fifth pulled themselves together as British heroes, threw off the power of the French, and saw Waterloo through. And when, on his return to England, one of that regiment was asked how the Battle of Waterloo was won, he said, using the same phrase that Nelson used nine years before: "By every man blazing away at his own gun."

We are in for a bigger fight than ever Waterloo was, against a better entrenched foe than ever the French were, and *this* battle is to be won by every man blazing away at his own gun.

And what is your gun? It is yourself. *You* are the gun.

And what is your powder? It is your own personal influence.

And what is your shot? It is your own personal endeavour.

And what is your fire? Without fire the gun and the powder and the shot are only an encumbrance. The fire is that love of God and of men which is generated in the heart of every one who believes that God so loved the world as to give His only begotten Son that whosoever believeth on Him should not perish, but have everlasting life.

When I realise what that love means to my own life, how God in Jesus Christ loved me and gave Himself for me, I cannot but feel that that love acts as fire on my personal influence so that it drives forth my personal endeavour to aim at some point for purity of life, and gain some victory over the corrupting influences of our time. Love of God and love of our fellow men, *that is fire!* Every man who wants to blaze away at his own gun in doing exploits in this

184

TEMPERANCE WATERLOO must have that fire. It will drive him out into Good Samaritanship. And, Good Samaritanship, working, working, among the fallen at our doors, and entering in through the gates of Congress into the doors of our legislators' hearts, will secure for us the Greater Waterloo for which this country cries aloud to-day.

Perhaps you ask: "If I am a gun, what am I to aim at? What is my target?" If you do ask this question, will you ask yourself another? Here it is: "Do I not know a drinker?" Please think what answer you can give to this question. Do you not know many drinkers? Have you ever tried to speak a word of warning to one of them? *Is it possible that you know two or three of your fellow-beings who are playing with damnation, and that you have never been so brave as to try to save even one of them from entering into it?* That drinker, whom you know, is your target. Aim at that target. Try to gain one point for God and purity of life by seeking, in the fight against drink, to save one fellow man or woman from the grip of the glass.

Would you like to save a brother or sister from destruction? I am sure you would. Allow me to say to you what an Irish priest said to me: "I have come to see that I can't do anything to get the people to give up the drink unless I am a total abstainer myself." If you are not a total abstainer you might take the hint, and become a wonderful power for good among your fellows, and bring joy, not only to your own fireside and the firesides of your friends, but also to the angels of God and to the very heart of God Himself.

A butcher leads a bullock to the door of a slaughter-house. Will the beast walk in willingly and unconcernedly? No! He will smell the blood of his slain brother in there before him, and he will stand back! If we begin to rake up our family histories, there is not one of us who will not come very soon upon the bones of a father or mother, sister or brother, son or daughter, or some bosom friend, lying in a drunkard's grave. Before we enter one of these *human slaughter-houses* in the main streets and down the side streets, on the highways and byways of our towns and country-side, it would be well if we could put ourselves in the place of the bullock that we might back from thence. Then we would come, not letting a mere brute instinct assert itself in our bosoms, but the instinct of human brotherhood and sisterhood, and, *smelling the blood of our slain brothers and sisters in there before us, we would, with the fire of heaven's wrath in our nostrils, stand back!* And, standing back ourselves, we should see it to be our duty to do all that in us lies to induce our fellows to stand back too. If we would all stand on the outside of the saloons there would soon be no inside for us to enter. The outside is the only safe side. For God and Home and country let us stand on the safe side.

Why are there so many publicans in the country? *Why are there so many shoemakers?* Just because there are so many people who want boots and shoes. If we all went barefoot, there would soon not be a shoemaker in the country. *Why are there so many bakers?* Because there are so many who eat bread. If we all decided to live on grass like Nebuchadnezzer, there would soon be not a baker in the country. *Why are there so many milliners?* Because the ladies all have such a desire to cover their beautiful adornment of natural hair by the wonderful productions of art we see everywhere—indeed we can hardly see anything else wherever they are! If all the ladies would make up their minds to let nature have a chance, there would soon be not a milliner in the country. *Why are there so many saloon-keepers?* Because there are so many people who want drink. And if we all made up our minds to do without drink, and to do everything in our power to promote the cause of total abstinence among our friends, there would soon be not a saloon-keeper in the country.

If, by a great pledge signing campaign, followed by a crusade of Good Samaritanship among those who have fallen half-dead at the hand of the drink thief, we could so much reduce the volume of drinking that those who are at present in the trade began to find it did not pay to continue in it, it is only reasonable to suppose that as they pass away, it will not be considered worth while on the part of others to take their places. Surely this end can be accomplished? Surely, if all the church-going people would take this crusade into their own hands they could so stagger the trade by a reduction in drinking as to make those who are engaged in it, saloon-keepers, brewers and distillers, wish to get out of it. And when we have succeeded in doing this, we shall not be far from our Greater Waterloo. It can be done by every man blazing away at his gun, and every woman too. And I am glad to know that the women of America are demanding and getting the power to vote. For when the women make up their minds *America's Waterloo* will soon be won.

CHAPTER XXXIV

Public Opinion: What Does Uncle Sam Say?

WE have always been told that we cannot legislate ahead of public opinion. If we ask for aggressive legislation it is only by public opinion we can ask it. If we have not got aggressive legislation it is because we have not an aggressive public opinion. One of the chief aims of the Catch-my-Pal crusade is to form that aggressive public opinion against which the gates of hell and the gates of our Legislature shall not be able to stand.

We get out of Parliament just what we put into it, and nothing more. We do not get the right legislation out because we do not put the right men in. We do not put the right men in because we have not a proper public opinion to seek them out and insist on their return to Parliament. When our public opinion is right we will put the right legislators into Parliament, and we shall get the right legislation out of it.

How are we going to seek out and return the right men? Simply by getting the people to take such an interest in each other's welfare that they will see their welfare is being ever threatened while human slaughter-houses are tolerated in their midst.

Why are these houses tolerated?

(1) Because there are so many people who drink moderately, and who give their support to the drink trade every time they take their glass.

(2) Because there are so many who drink to excess and give excessive support to the trade.

(3) Because there are so many total abstainers who,

while they withhold their support from the trade. as far as cash is concerned, are indirectly helping it by their utter indifference to the results of the moderate and excessive drinking of their fellows.

(a) The trade smiles on the moderate drinkers as its best customers, seeing that they are still respectable.

(b) The trade may have regrets about the excessive drinkers as they debauch themselves at its bar, but it throws them out as soon as it has secured their cash.

(c) The trade laughs at the total abstainers who, while they take good care to keep out of its clutches themselves, have no care for those who are already in those clutches.

While the majority in any community is composed of these three classes, those who play with the drink, those who are its slaves, and those who don't care, so long. will the saloons stand at our corners and along our streets and highways, belching out their vulgar, up-roarious horse-laughter at all attempts to undermine them and their nefarious business.

The Catch-my-Pal method of attack on the saloon is this: It urges total abstainers, especially professing Christians, to wake up and realise that, after all, total abstinence is a very small thing on the part of any person if it does not lead to personal interest in those who are not abstainers. It seeks to arouse the sense of individual responsibility, so that those who know the blessings of total abstinence will become mission-aries of these blessings to those about them who need these blessings most. And, when a great drinker is saved by the personal interest and endeavour of a total abstainer, it sends that reclaimed drinker out as *the best possible missionary* to his pals who are still drink-ing. When a number of these great drinkers come to-gether along the lines of sobriety into a brotherhood, they soon form a public opinion among themselves, which becomes to them the mainstay of their reformed life. Then the moderate drinker, seeing how the no-

torious drinker whom he formerly despised has the
manhood to go past the saloon, begins to think it is
nearly time he began to follow his example, and pass
it too.

The FIRST MOVE is made by the total abstainer
towards his fallen brother. This fallen one becomes
in his new life a missionary to his pals. And, when
a number of them become leagued together in the
new life of sobriety, the moderate drinkers begin to
pull themselves up through very shame. While it is
usually a total abstainer who starts the work of reform
in any locality, *the most effective development of it
falls into the hands of the hard drinkers.* This has
been so abundantly proved throughout the country
wherever this movement has had a chance that I am
more and more inclined to lay stress on the statement
I made to the first six men, "Let those who make the
problem solve it." Every drinker saved, especially if
he has been a great drinker, becomes immediately:
(1) An object of curiosity; (2) an object lesson; and
(3) an object of solicitude to the whole community
in which he lives; and the natural desire of all who
know him is that all occasion of stumbling in future
may be taken out of his way. Local public opinion
begins to focus itself on the saloon, and the local option is that the occasion of stumbling at the corner
should be removed, at least for the reclaimed one's
sake.

When a great number of drinkers are reclaimed,
the local desire for the closing of the saloon becomes
all the more intense. It is our aim, therefore, to hasten
the reclamation of the drinkers by Good Samaritanship, so that we may intensify the desire for local option or prohibition, and hasten the putting into operation of the means whereby that desire may be realised.
Good Samaritanship, a sense of interest in the rescued,
and a feeling of shame on the part of moderate drinkers, these, together with the educative forces at work,

are the chief determining factors in the formation of a
local public opinion against the local saloon; and the
Catch-my-Pal movement aims at such a development
of these factors in all localities as shall result in the
return to Parliament and to local councils of those candidates only who will legislate on local option lines, or
who will pledge themselves to action in, and not to
mere sympathy with, the crusade against the trade.

Let me give a concrete example of Catch-my-Pal
methods in seeking to obtain local prohibition. In a
certain district the movement gathered into its membership about two thousand men, among whom were
many who had been formerly considered hopeless
drinkers. An election was about to take place. The
candidate made his statement at a public meeting, and
promised to be sympathetic with temperance reform.
The chairman said he supposed they were all satisfied
with what the candidate had said. The Secretary
of the Catch-my-Pal Union said that there was a depu-
tation from the Union present, and in the name of
the Union they wished to state that they had been
content too long with getting "sympathy" from their
representatives. They now wanted action. They
wanted their candidate to promise to vote for local
option, no matter by what party it was introduced into
the House of Commons. The candidate hesitated,
but when he received a hint that if he did not consent
there would probably be two thousand votes in the
balance, he consented to vote for local option, and
expressed his consent in writing. *If we cannot find
members of Parliament who will vote for prohibition
because of their own consciences, we must see that we
return members who must vote for it because of the
conscience of their constituencies.*

THIS IS NOT A PARTY PROBLEM. It is a problem for
all parties in the States. It is a question that must be
lifted above all party interests in our State legislatures
and in Congress. We must see that we will not

be a party to the giving of honour to the man who buttresses by his vote the trade which brings our sons and daughters to dishonour. *Every candidate should be squared on this question before he appears on the hustings at all.* After a candidate is chosen to fight a constituency he may promise almost anything to secure his own return, and as soon as the fight is over and he stands in the House, he may fail to stand by the promises he made in the heat of the election. His conscience gives its heels to his personal and party vanity as a MEMBER OF THE HOUSE!

Is it not possible to develop such a public conscience and opinion in each constituency that no candidate for parliamentary honours will think of putting himself forward, and no official delegates who, in the name of the constituency, choose the candidate, will think of bringing any candidate forward, unless he is prepared to vote according to the public conscience of the constituency on this question? All parties in a constituency should aim at such a development of public opinion in their constituency that *the successful candidate will be the right man on this question, no matter what his party politics may be.* Morley says of Gladstone: "He was steadfast for making politics more human, and no branch of civilised life needs humanising more." This drink question is a political question, but it is not a party political one. It is one over which all parties can shake hands across the House and say: "This is not a party question—*it is a question of common humanity*, and we will all unite our hands and hearts in 'seeing this thing through.'"

We want local prohibition. Some people want national prohibition. I would accept national prohibition to-day if I could get it. But I consider that *the best way to secure national prohibition is along local prohibition lines*. We can never have national prohibition till the people are aroused to prohibit, and if localities are so aroused as to clamour for local prohibition the nation will be aroused to clamour for more in the form of national prohibition.

We want local prohibition. We cannot have it without legislation. We cannot have legislation without public opinion. The best way to form public opinion is to organise a campaign of Good Samaritanship among the victims of drink. *We should never ask our representatives to do within the doors of the Legislature what we refuse to take off our coats to do at our own doorstep.* There is a man in the drunken gutter. Five minutes of well directed thought, sympathy, and brotherhood may save that man even though there never was a syllable of temperance legislation in the statute book of the United States. Why should I ask my representative to do by legislation what I will not personally touch with one of my fingers? Let me rather first go out and lift up my fallen brother. Then, having shown I am in earnest I can demand that my representative in Parliament shall give his influence and vote for the passing of such legislation as shall take the stumbling-block out of my brother's way. Let all who name the name of Christ and say they love God love their neighbours as themselves, and show their love by the self-sacrifice that goes out to save the lost, and there will soon be developed over the land an opinion against the saloon which no Government can afford to neglect. Such public opinion will find its way through the doors of the State Legislatures and will express itself in such a way as to convince the legislators that it is the voice of God, and *the drink trade will tremble to its foundations when it hears the voice of God before the Speaker's chair.*

If the PEOPLE manifest a desire to be freed from a bondage that galls their life and grinds their children, the voice of the people becomes the very voice of God, and our legislators will hear and understand and act. All true social legislation is but the embodiment and codification of the people's will, as expressed through their representatives. That will has shown itself in the many legislative acts which have been passed to *regulate* the drink traffic, but it has never yet been so strong as to go to Congress and demand the destruction of the destroyer. Now, we want its destruction. It is not a high ideal to aim merely at regulating the destruction of the people. *Surely the destroyer must be destroyed and not regulated?* How is this to be accomplished? By the will of the people. Are the people willing? *That* is the question. We must not first ask if the Legislature is willing. That is a secondary question, but it is one we are fond of asking, because behind it we think we can hide our own individual and communal responsibility. We say we want legislation, and that our legislators are so slow. And, while we are waiting for legislation to come and lift our fallen brother out of the gutter, our brother is lost—*lost, not so much by want of legislation as by want of brotherhood. We* might have saved him without legislation. This is one of the thoughts at the heart of the Catch-my-Pal movement. And when it has done its work, by welding the community into one vast brotherhood for the salvation of those who are down, people will be able to go to Congress and demand an Act of Congress as an Act of the People, by which it will be made *impossible for temptation to stand in a legalised capacity at the corners of our streets.*

The Son of God was manifested to *destroy* the works of the devil. Can the drink demon not be slain? Can the work of the drink devil not be destroyed? Can we find no way of compassing his craftiness? *Must we still be "bossed" by the beer jug?* Is the drink traffic still to stand at its doors with arms akimbo, and laughing at all attempts by a Christian nation to take its life?

One day a Scotch farmer was going out over his fields, and he saw a little man walking over his potato rigs, trampling down the plants without any regard to the damage he was doing. The farmer approached him and said:

"What are ye doin' walkin' o'er ma potato rigs? Tak yersel' oot o' this."

The wee man said with an air of offended official-dom:

"Do you know whom you are talking to?"

"I dinna care wha I'm talkin' tae, I'll no alloo ony man tae walk o'er ma potato rigs; tak yersel' oot o' this!"

"Do you know that I am a Government man?"

"I dinna care whether ye're a Government man or no, I tell ye I'll no alloo ony man to walk o'er ma potato rigs; tak yersel oot o' this!"

"Well, if you don't believe I am a Government man I'll show you my Government papers."

The farmer went off to his yard and brought out a great bull with a ring in his nose, and a tether in the ring. He took the tether out of the ring and directed the bull's attention to the wee Government man. Away the bull went after the wee Government man with bent neck, fiery nostrils and erect tail. Away the wee Government man went for the nearest dyke he could find! And the farmer, making a trumpet with his hands, shouted after him:

"Haigh, ma wee Government man, will ye show him yer Government paper-r-r-r-rs!"

The drink trade comes out and stalks about over the land, trampling down our country's prosperity, irrespective of what damage it is doing as long as it serves its own ends. We approach it and ask: "What are you doing, trampling down the prosperity of our country in such a fashion?" It says: "Do you know whom you are talking to? Do you know that I am a Government institution? Do you not know that I have got Government papers? Do you not know that I am a licensed trade? If you don't believe me I'll show you my papers. Here is my license. What have you got to say to that?" Licensed to do what? *Licensed to damn the·women! Licensed to starve the children! Licensed to fill our workhouses! Licensed to send twenty-five per cent. of the inmates to our asylums! Licensed to make the worst of our city slumdom! Licensed to increase lust! Licensed to make murderers! Licensed to empty our churches! Licensed to make hell at the fireside! Licensed to turn the mightiest intellects into gibbering idiots! Licensed to send men and women made in the image of God down to the lowest·depths of hell's perdition! Licensed to crush the heart of the Man of Sorrows! Licensed to break up the partnership between God and man in the making of a new earth!*

Yet that trade has the brazen effrontery of hell in standing and flouting its license before the faces of Americans and demanding: "What have you to say to THAT?"

In America, if you wish to know what public opinion is, you ask: "What does Uncle Sam say?". On the other side of the Atlantic, if you wish to know what British public opinion is, you ask: "What does John Bull say?" And when the drink trade pushes its license into their faces and asks what they have to say to *that,* it is for Britishers to form a public opinion, called John Bull, and to let THAT out at this licensed damnation, and drive it from their land.

China made up her mind in 1906, and expressed her mind in an Imperial Decree, that she would drive the opium curse out of her land, and solve her opium problem in ten years. I understand that already about seventy-five per cent. of the opium dens are closed.

If the nation which we used to speak of with a sneer ·of "heathen Chinee" on our lips can rise and perform such an exploit, it is time that the leading Christian nations should rise and do their duty.

And we shall never do our duty at the ballot-box

if we are not willing to do our duty to our fallen brethren. If there was an attempt to drive the thieves off the road between Jerusalem and Jericho by means of legislation, no reliance could be placed on either the priest or the Levite in bringing that legislation about. The priest would take no interest in the solution of the problem because he took no interest in saving the person. The Levite would take no interest in solving the problem because he took no interest in saving the person. But, on the day of the ballot, commend to me the Samaritan. He took an interest in the person. He went out of his way to save the man at the wayside, and he would go out of his way to vote to drive the thief from the highway.

If I pass the drunkard or drinker by I'll take little interest in the drink problem. But if I go out of my way to save the drunkard I'll also go out of my way to vote to destroy the drunkard-maker. If we go to the trouble to study the damnation caused by drink we'll rise in all our God-given might and bring damnation to the drink. *GOOD SAMARITANSHIP IS THE KEY TO THE SOLUTION OF THE DRINK PROBLEM.*

CHAPTER XXXV

What Are the Churchgoers Doing?

HUMAN nature has an instinct for ritual in almost every sphere of life, and especially in the religious sphere. In the early church whose members were formerly Jews, accustomed to Old Testament ritual, there would naturally be a sort of hankering after that ritual. These Christians could hardly be expected to be quite reconciled to the new way of worship that did away practically with all ceremonies of a ritualistic type. And so St. James says to such Christians, "Pure religion and undefiled before God the Father means this: to care for orphans and widows in their trouble, and to keep oneself from the stain of the world." The word here translated "religion" does not mean a system of doctrine or an adherence to a particular creed. It means rather *religious ceremonial*. And the advice of the apostle to these early Christians might be paraphrased in this way: If you want religious ceremonial and ritual you can have as much as you want by keeping yourselves free from the sin of the world, and living differently from the worldly people, and by caring for (Dr. Moffatt says the word implies *personal* service and help) orphans and widows; in other words, looking after the fallen, and seeking to solve the social questions of the day.

Is there not a strong word here for the Churchgoers of to-day? What treading of the courts of Christian temples! What forms and ceremonies! What ritual! What meetings! What singing of hymns! What tasting of Sermons! What enjoyments

of Intellectual Treats! What Organ Recitals! What
genuflections! What repetitions of prayers! What
attendance at Church for appearance's sake! What
Churchianity! And, over against all these, what orphans and widows and derelicts! And what institu-
tions, licensed for the making of orphans and widows
and derelicts! LICENSED BY THE CHRISTIAN
COMMUNITY!

What effect have the hymn-singing and the praying
and the sermon tasting and the intellectual treats on
the continuance or discontinuance of these licensed
destroyers?

In Scotland, if you want to know who is a person's
minister, you will likely ask him, "What minister do
you SIT under?" The very common idea of the end
and aim of Church attendance entertained by many
Christian people is embodied in that question. A lady
was one day passing along a road by the side of which
an old blind man had sat for many years begging. She
stopped and asked him, "I have often wondered how
you pass your time on this bench?" And he answered,
"Well, ma'am, sometimes I sits and I thinks, and
sometimes I JUST SITS."

How characteristic of so many churchgoers!

> They sit and they sit and they sit and they sit
> And they sit and they sit and they sit;
> They sit and they sit and they sit and they sit,
> And they sit and they sit and they sit!

There would be more hope of a speedy victory over
the forces of evil if the question was put in this way:

WHAT MINISTER DO YOU *GO* UNDER?

While we see outside many churches that "A Hearty
welcome is given to all," the welcome cannot come
from the bell tower or from the well carpeted aisle, or
from the comfortable pew, or from the wood of the
pulpit, or from any part of the mere fabric of the

church building. The welcome must come from the CHURCH, *from the PEOPLE in the church.* And that welcome to the outcast and the downcast, and to those on the highways and by the hedges, must be given by the people of the church GOING to extend the welcome. We must go out into the highways and hedges and compel them to come in by self-sacrifice, by good Samaritanship. *The Man half dead cannot COME. We must Go to him And if there was more Going on the part of the Church to the World, there. would be. more Coming on the part of the World to the Church.*

No one can find fault with the *Christianity of Christ,* but there is much wrong with the *Churchianity of the Churches.*

If the Christianity of Christ was allowed to displace the Churchianity. of the Churches there would be the greatest revolution and revival the world has ever seen.

The Churches have been settling down into snug and smug and respectable societies for *preserving the preserved,* instead of being aggressive missionary societies going out to seek and save the lost, *lost within sight of the churches!*

The wealthy congregation engages a missionary and sends him on a bread and butter salary to work in the slums. He goes down among the outcasts and teaches half starved, half naked, filthy little children to sing,

"There is a happy land *far, far* away."

If the people in that congregation would work personally, and not by deputy, they would come to realise the problem of the slum in such a way that they would rise in all their wealth and social prestige and religious fervour and form a public opinion that would solve the problem, and let the little children see and enjoy the "happy land" *here* and *now.* We thank God for all those who pray and act as they pray; for all those who sing with all their heart and act as they sing; for all those who taste sermons and go out with the messages of the sermons to the world; and for all those who can and do enjoy intellectual treats and go and reduce these intellectual things to the simplicity that can be understood by the unlearned among whom they labour much in love. But, notwithstanding all these people of God who are the salt of the earth, is there not room for some questions like the following :—

How many thousands sing,

> "Rescue the perishing, care for the dying,
> Snatch them in pity from sin and the grave."

How many of those who sing these words go out to rescue the perishing, to care for the dying, snatching them in pity from sin and the grave? Can those who sing these words, and *do nothing,* not be taught the ritualism recommended by St. James? *Go and Do Something!* Then, what thousands sing,

> "Onward Christian soldiers,
> Marching as to war."

And how many of those thousands go out of the church and lie behind the baggage all the week, afraid to take or make any stand for Jesus or to venture forth against the enemy! I have heard this hymn sung for many years, and *we are not done marching yet!* Indeed, it seems as if the march was hardly organised yet. But when is the WAR to begin? Is the enemy in sight yet? If he is in sight, and surely he is, then why all this marching? Is it not nearly time the fighting had begun? Had the Rev. S. Baring Gould a drop of sarcasm on the point of his pen when he wrote the second line of his hymn? Are we marching to war? Or are we merely "marching *as to* war"? Is it a case of BLUFF? Is the Church in earnest? If she is why does she sing,

"Stand up, stand up, for Jesus,
The strife will not be long;
This day the noise of battle,
The next the victor's song."

What noise of battle is there to-day? Is it not *the still small voice of a whispering compromise* we hear? The strife has not yet begun in earnest. How is it that the strife will not be long? Where do we hear the song of the victor who is more than conqueror. against the rulers of the darkness of this world? Why is it that there are so many misgivings about the "victory" of Christianity even in professedly Christian lands?

How many thousands in our churches sing,

"I LOVE TO TELL THE STORY,"

and how many of those thousands never open their lips to tell the story they sing they LOVE to tell?

How many thousands of Churchgoers are quite content to sing,

"Lord, Thou hast here Thy ninety and nine;
Are they not enough for Thee?"

If they do not mean this by their words, do they not show that they mean this by their action, or, rather, INACTION? Imagine any mother who has ten children, and one of them is a lovely girl walking the streets of Chicago, "far off from the gates of gold" that open to the family circle in a Christian home. Imagine some other woman coming to that mother to comfort her by saying, "Sure, you have here nine of your children. *Are they not enough for you?*" Could a more damnable insult be cast into the face of motherhood? And yet, how many churchgoers by their inaction throw that insult into the face of Jesus Christ!

WHAT ARE CHURCHGOERS DOING?

How many thousands of Churchgoers kneel down and pray,

"Thy Kingdom come"

They pray "Thy kingdom come" with their lips on Sunday, and on Monday they set their teeth against the Kingdom's coming.

I venture to say that the great obstacle to the progress of the Christian Church to-day is not the drink-traffic; it is not white slavery; it is not gambling; it is not any specific presumptuous sin: THE GREATEST OBSTACLE TO THE PROGRESS OF THE CHARIOT WHEELS OF THE KINGDOM OF GOD IS THE *ABSOLUTE INDIFFERENCE OF THE MAJORITY OF THE PEOPLE IN THE CHURCHES.*

I venture to say that about seven-tenths of the people in the churches, apart from singing and praying and listening to sermons, are indifferent to the world's salvation. Most of them think of their own selfish salvation, and as long as they think they can get into heaven by the skin of their own teeth, they are inclined to let the rest of their creed run like, "let the devil take the hindmost."

I venture to say that if churchgoers acted as they sing and pray the world would be turned upside down in a generation.

I venture to say that the most awful statement I ever heard was this, repeated by a great and good minister in England at a missionary conference, *"Some time ago a Chinese gentleman said he did not want his son to become a Christian, and he thought the best way to prevent him from becoming a Christian was to send him to a Christian country, for there he would see such things tolerated in the name of Christianity as would prevent him from ever thinking of changing his creed."*

I venture to say that there is not much encouragement in our Christian civilisation to the heathen nations to accept our civilisation, when they see our saloons and slums, and know all about our white slavery and all about the ten thousand abominations that are associated with our drink-traffic.

I venture to say that *the best way to accomplish missionary work abroad is to purify our Christian civilisation at home.* If the Christian people and churchgoers at home would go out to seek and save the lost, to rescue the perishing and to care for the dying, and, by self-sacrifice, come to an understanding of the causes of all the abominations with which our civilisation is cursed, they would rise and form such a public opinion as would remove these causes in a "strife" that would "not be long." If churchgoers who profess the Name of Christ would show the Spirit of Christ by going out to save the fallen in a great campaign of Good Samaritanship, and, by so doing, solve the drink problem, drive immorality from our streets, remove the slums, and make our Christian civilisation what it ought to be *and can be,* there would be such a revolution at home as the world has never seen, and the heathen nations would come flocking to us and saying, "If this thing called Christianity can do this for these people, if it can make them so happy, so pure, so clean, so moral, so quite unlike and so far ahead of all the rest of the people in the world, then THIS IS THE THING FOR US. WE CANNOT AFFORD TO BE WITHOUT THIS THING CALLED CHRISTIANITY." It is the spirit of sacrifice that can do this thing for our civilisation,—Christian self-sacrifice. And when that Spirit is manifested by those who profess the Name of Jesus Christ, then will be fulfilled the words of Jesus, "And I, if I be lifted up from the earth, will draw all men unto Myself." It is for the Church to lift up Jesus Christ by shewing the world His Spirit of Self-sacrifice. And every one who shews that spirit by going down among the fallen and the outcast is doing his part in purifying our Christian society, and in helping to form that public opinion that will rise and by one fell sweep brush from before our eyes those licensed evils that have so long been a stench in the nostrils of God and a stumbling-block in the way of the heathen to the heart of Jesus Christ.

The churches must set in motion and keep in motion the machinery for the formation of public opinion: They are in the world to do the work of Jesus Christ; and the world looks to them for Good Samaritanship:

It cannot be denied that many people in all the churches are doing splendid work in lifting the fallen and bringing in the outcast, and that many congregations are so imbued with the spirit of Jesus Christ that they devote their best energies to missionary work at home and abroad. At the same time it cannot be denied that the great majority of churchgoers take but little interest in the solution of the ugly social problems lying about our very church doors.

If you ask the members of our churches: "What do you go to church for?" some will answer; "I go to church to worship God." Others will give other answers. But most people will say: "I go to church to get good." I have been hearing church-going people say this all through my ministry, and *I often wonder what in all the world people do with all the good they get.* They go to church to "get good" and they blame the minister if he preaches "too long"; and, possibly, once in a while he is blamed if he preaches "too short." Then the elders and deacons and church-wardens and class-leaders are blamed if there is a church draught. And who ever heard of a church without a draught? Men go home and talk for a whole week about the evil effects of that draught on the backs of their heads, but they never say a word about the effect of the sermon on their hearts. Why?

Because it is difficult to talk of a thing that does not exist. We all know how, when the minister is shooting shafts of truth from the pulpit to pierce the hearts of the people with the sense of individual responsibility, the instinct of self-preservation goes out in front of almost every person in the pews. That instinct takes the form of a double-sided shield. The first shaft hits the right side of the shield and glints off to the right. The second shaft hits the left side and glints off to the left, while the person behind the shield follows those shafts to the hearts of his neighbours, and he says: "Now they are getting it! The minister is touching them up now! Oh, isn't he giving it to them to-day?"

I was going down the street with a County Antrim elder one Sunday after the morning service. He said:

"You had some plain talk in your sermon to-day."

"I suppose I had," I answered.

"Yes, and do you know," he added: "there were a great many people there to-day who were badly in need of it."

All the time I was talking "plainly" in the sermon, that elder was sitting in the pew behind his little shield saying: "Now they are getting it; now they are getting it!" And when an elder says so, one can excuse an ordinary body!

"What good do I do on Monday with the good I get in church on Sunday?" is a question worthy of the earnest attention of all church goers, especially of communicants. Most people who go to church acknowledge that they are Christians. If any of them was told he was not a Christian he would probably say: "Don't insult me!" A Christian is a Christ-one, one who follows in the steps of Christ. A fair test of one's Christianity might be made by each church goer asking himself or herself on Saturday night such questions as these: "I went to church last Sunday to get good:

WHAT ARE CHURCHGOERS DOING?

"(1) Did I, a professed follower of Christ, LIFT UP a fallen brother or sister during the past six days?

"(2) Did I, a professed follower of Christ, TRY TO LIFT UP a fallen brother or sister during the past six days?

"(3) Did I, a professed follower of Christ, during the past six days, EVEN PRAY THAT I MIGHT BE ENABLED TO LIFT UP OR TO TRY TO LIFT UP a fallen brother or sister?"

These questions must be answered some day. On *"that day,"* when we all stand before the Great White Throne, no church member will be able to cast his personal responsibility on to the shoulders of other people. There will be no shuffling on that day, and it would be better for us to square with God to-day by doing our duty than have God to square with us on that day after we have failed to do our duty.

Our Lord went to church on Sundays. "As His custom was He went into the synagogue on the Sabbath day." He got good there. Heaven was about Him there on the Sabbath day. He went away into the desert alone with The Infinite Purity, and He got good there. He went up the mountains apart to pray, and He got good there. But, what did He do with the good He got? That is the question for Christians.

He came out of the synagogue; back from the desert; down from the mountain; and He went away down into the valleys of sin and shame and debauchery and death that He might DO GOOD. *He went about doing good.* He could talk well. Never man spake like this Man. But He practised what He preached. He never walked on the primrose path of dalliance. If He talked well He *did* all things well, and left us an example that we might follow *IN HIS STEPS.*

If any church goer has not the spirit of Christ he is none of His. We may go to church on Sunday to get good, and to sing our psalms and hymns and

207

spiritual songs; to criticise the ministers and taste the sermons; to test draughts and draw long faces, and to say, "Lord, Lord," but if we consider church attendance and public religious ceremony as ends and not as means, they are mere ritual. The ceremonial of public worship is very necessary, but it has to be kept in its place as only one of the ways we try to express our religion; it must not be put in the place of religion. If we spend our religious energies in religious ceremonial and let life's opportunities for service pass by, it is possible the church's Lord will say to us on that day: "You spent your time in calling Me, Lord, Lord, but you did not the things which I said, for, inasmuch as ye did it not to one of the least of these, My brethren, ye did it not to Me. Depart from Me; I never knew you."

I am sure there never were more Good Samaritans in the world than there are to-day. There never was a greater desire in the heart of the Christian community to save the fallen than there is to-day. But there is not yet so much of the spirit of self-sacrifice in our churches as is necessary to save the country as we desire it to be saved. Our church gathers at the Communion Table to show forth there the Lord's sacrifice till He come. *But while so many of us who show forth His sacrifice at the table go from the table and show no sacrifice of ourselves, it is no wonder the Lord is so long in coming.*

God says: "I will have mercy and not sacrifice." He cannot away with our sacrifices in church if they are mere ceremonies. How can He accept our sacrifices of praise and prayer in church, if on our way to church we refuse to show mercy? If I saw my neighbour's beast in a ditch when on my way to church I believe I could keep the Sabbath better by stopping to show mercy at the ditch than by going on to the altar to pray. And, if I must feel constrained to give attention to my neighbour's beast, how can I dare to stand before God if I pass by my neighbour's self?

The Church has science on her side, and the sense of brotherhood, sisterhood, fatherhood, motherhood. She has the sense of an invincible right on her side. She has the sense of having tolerated this licensed curse long enough, too long, on her side. She has the sense of the vision of a new era on her side. And with all these on our side, we can, by the example of Jesus and the inspiration of His Spirit, arise and weld and pummel and shape a public opinion which nothing can stand against. Public opinion is sometimes misguided and sometimes impulsive, but finally it finds the path which is eminently right, and then, in a God-given zeal, it can sweep all opposition before it and claim the community for purity of life.

CHAPTER XXXVI

A Word to the Moderate Drinker

I HAVE said in another place that the Moderate Drinker is the greatest curse in the country, as far as this drink problem is concerned. If I were a saloon-keeper I should not wish to have queues of drunkards about my bar door. They would disgrace me and my trade. But I should like to have crowds of moderate drinkers about my door. A moderate drinker is one who can take a little drop now, and a little drop again, and another little drop at another time, and two or three other little drops at two or three other little times, and yet never appear under the influence of drink or get into the hands of the police. *This man is the mainstay of the drink trade.* Every time he goes into a bar and orders a drink, and pays for it, he is doing his part to keep on its feet financially the greatest curse that walks our streets. He gives his moral support to the greatest instrument of immorality in the land. He makes it possible for the curse to continue its temptations to the unwary and its destruction of those who are already in its clutches.

But the Moderate Drinker says, "I'll not be muzzled. Why should I put a muzzle on my mouth? I don't believe in pledges." A good dog is worth muzzling when there is poison about. No one is anxious about a mongrel pup. I should like to place every man in the category of the "good dogs" that are worth saving. When I was in Trinity College, Dublin, I heard men say they did not believe in being muzzled. But they are muzzled to-day. Their muzzles measure six feet by three, for they are in drunkards' graves!

When a man asks a girl to be his wife he asks her to take a pledge, and he takes a pledge at the same time himself. If a man takes a pledge to be true and faithful to one woman, and plights his troth in the most public way at the marriage altar, he cannot excuse himself from taking another pledge, the keeping of which will help him to be more faithful to the one he took on his marriage day.

The Moderate Drinker excuses his moderation by saying that he drinks for the good of his country, as it is necessary to derive revenue from the drink trade to run the finances of the country. But apart altogether from the financial aspect of the question, and the fact that the country spends much more on dealing with the results of drink than she derives from the sale of it, the moderate drinker should be honest and confess that he does not drink because he loves his country, but simply because he loves the drink. He never thought of the benefit his drink was to the country when he was at the bar. His only regret was that his throat was not about a mile and a half long that he might have enjoyed the drink all the more while it was going down. The moderate drinker does not drink for the revenue of his country, but for the revenue of hell. Isaiah says regarding the drinkers, "Therefore hell hath enlarged herself and opened her mouth without measure: and their glory and their multitude and their pomp, and he that rejoiceth shall descend into it." The moderate drinker is a drunkard in the making, and no drunkard shall inherit the kingdom of heaven.

The Moderate Drinker says, "But, you see, I can take it or let it alone." I have heard many men say this who are in drunkards' graves to-day. The moderate drinker thinks he is playing with the drink, while it is really the drink that is playing with him. When a man says, "I can take it or let it alone," and if he keeps on taking it, we know that the first part of his statement is true. But what about the second part of it? If he would only let it alone we should then know that he could let it alone; but when he keeps on taking it we begin to think that it has so fascinated him he cannot let it alone. To every drinker who says, "I can let it alone," I say, *"Well, let it alone and then I'll know that you CAN."*

The Moderate Drinker says, "I take only a little drop." Well, then, moderate drinker, it will be all the lesser sacrifice if you give it up. I have great sympathy with heavy drinkers who are asked to take the pledge. It must be a terrible wrench to them, from the crown of the head to the sole of their feet, to give up the drink and conquer the craving for it. It is indeed a sacrifice that means blood. But I have no sympathy with the drinker who says he takes only a little drop and who has not the manliness to make the sacrifice of that little drop, for the sake of a wife, or a mother, or a daughter, or a son, or a father, or a lover. And I would advise every girl, when asked to become a wife, to ask her suitor if he is a total abstainer. If he says he is not, she should ask him to give up the glass for her sake. He will then have to *choose between his glass and his girl,* and if he will not give up the glass for his girl's sake, and at her request, he will show that he loves his glass better than he loves his girl, and she should have nothing to do with him. I have known many girls who ventured to marry moderate drinkers in the hope of weaning them from the drink, and those girls found hell at their firesides before they were long in the married life.

I would appeal to the moderate drinker to give up the little drop lest that little drop might lead to a great drop on the part of another. You, a moderate drinker, meet a young fellow in the street. You knew his father. You ask him to come with you to have a talk over "old times." He goes with you, and he finds you are bringing him into a saloon. He hesitates at the door and says he does not go into such places. But you urge him. He still holds back, for he feels as if some one was tugging at the collar of his jacket and urging him not to go in. He hears his father's voice saying, "Don't go in! Don't go in!" But you still urge him, and again he hesitates, for he hears the yearning voice of his mother saying into his ear, "Don't go in! Oh! My boy, my boy, don't go in. Don't go in!" But you still induce him. You SE-DUCE him in. He goes in. You and he sit down, and you ask him, "What will you have?" He says, "A bottle of lemonade." You say, "Oh, don't talk non-sense; take something stronger." He says, "But, I am a total abstainer." You say, "Oh, come along! None of your old wives' talk. Take a dram like the rest of us and be a MAN." You drop that insidious temptation into his ear and heart. He has come from the country side and he *begins to think it is a sign of manhood in the city* to take a drop like the rest of them. He falls before that appeal to his manhood, and you order his drink. He takes from YOUR HAND his FIRST DRINK. That first drink sets a-going within him the fires of hell, arouses a craving for drink he may have inherited from his grandfather. He begins there and then to go down the inclined plane of a drinker's life. He goes down with rattling glee to the drunkard's stage. He comes to the end of the drunkard's career, and drops into a drunkard's grave. You stand at his grave side and see his remains cov-ered in the earth. How do you feel? Do you think? Do you remember? Had you anything to do with the digging of that grave? Have you finished with him now? Is the transaction quite completed? Will you ever hear any more of that young man in the drunkard's grave? You must stand before the Great White Throne. The Judge will be on the throne.

And a man's lost soul will be there, the soul that you seduced at the saloon. That man will square you up before the throne. He will look at you with a lost soul's eyes. He will point at you with his finger. He will say to you with a voice that will be hell in your ears, "WOE, WOE unto him that putteth the bottle to his neighbour's lips! It was you, you; you!!! YOU!!!! YOU!!!!! who first put the bottle to my lips and set a-going these flames of hell within me. It was through YOU that I was led to take the first step that led me to a drunkard's life, a drunkard's grave, and a drunkard's doom, and I have come up from the depths of hell's perdition to square you up before the Great White Throne to-day, and to look into your face and call you, *damned! damned!! DAMNED!!!*"

Moderate drinker! Are you prepared to face THAT music on the great day? Will you not give up your *little drop*, lest it may lead to a *great drop* down to perdition on the part of a friend or the son of a friend?

The Son of God "poured out His soul unto death" for you. Will you not pour out that "little drop" and sacrifice *that much* for Him and for your brother, for whom also Christ died?

CHAPTER XXXVII

Brooks by the Way

I AM continually being asked by ministers and others, "When are you going back to the ministry? Are you not tired of this going about and being away so much from home? Would it not be better for you to settle down in a parish again?"

In answer to these queries I say, 1. I never left the ministry. I simply entered a larger ministry when I left Armagh. 2. I am tired of going about. It is a terrible drudgery. I hate it. It is very lonely to have none of one's own dear ones near for about ten months in the year. I long for home as much as any man ever did. But if I gave up this work I should be laying down my cross. If my being tired of being always on the road is the means of bringing some wanderer back to home from the broad road, I cannot take rest, lest resting might mean failing to save men and to make happy firesides. 3. If I settled down as a parish minister I should be choosing what appears to me, at any rate, the path of primroses as compared with my present path of thorns. I believe that if I came to the fork in the road, and chose to go by the path of primroses, all power of conveying blessing to men would there and then leave me, and the remainder of my life would be a failure. I could not expect Him, Who took up His Cross, to accompany me if I laid down my cross. Therefore I cannot see how, with a good conscience, I could go back to a settled pastorate.

I should have no hesitation in going back, if I thought my call to my present work had come to an end. But that it has not come to an end will appear from some experiences I give here.

Nearly everywhere I go I am told how helpful my message is. At the close of every meeting I address in America I receive such testimonies as to encourage me wonderfully to persevere. Many good folk who attend to their religious duties as church goers have testified and still testify of the stimulus my words have been and are to them in going out to do good.

A young lady told me recently that she never did any definite Christian work till she heard me speak. She then went out on fire to do something for her fallen brothers and sisters, and, so earnest did she become in the work, her friends said she was "Catch-my-Pal mad." She has been the means of doing wonderful things in her neighbourhood.

One night at the close of a meeting a lady came to me and said, "I am going away from this meeting perfectly miserable." And when I asked her why she said so she answered, "Till I heard you to-night I thought I was doing all that was necessary when I went regularly to church and attended to the services. But now I see how selfish I have been, and how many opportunities of doing good I have allowed to slip. And when I think of all that I might have done and of how little I have done, I am going away perfectly miserable." I said to her, "Well, madam, I am glad to hear that you are perfectly miserable, for I go on the platform to make people feel perfectly miserable till they go out to do something to lift up their fallen brothers and sisters. And I am going away perfectly happy because you are going away perfectly miserable; and I hope you will go and work off your misery by trying to make up for lost opportunities." She said she would try, and we parted.

Experiences such as these greatly encourage me to go on with the Catch-my-Pal crusade. But I have greater encouragements than these.

216

BROOKS BY THE WAY

I was going along the street one Sunday morning to preach in a church in Londonderry. A young man accosted me with a hearty "Good morning, Mr. Patterson." I asked him how he knew me. He said that he had been at the first meeting I held in Derry, and that he signed the pledge that night. I asked him if he had been a drunkard, and he said, "No, I was not a drunkard, but, judging by the way I was drinking it would not have been long till I'd have been a drunkard. I have taken no drink since I signed at your meeting three years ago."

I walked down the street about one hundred and fifty yards. An old stooped man met me. He said, "Good morning, your reverence." And I said, "How do you know me?" He looked up at me, and with a tremor in his voice he said, "I have a good right to know you. My wife and I signed the pledge at your first meeting in Derry three years ago." I asked if they had been drinkers, and he said they were both heavy drinkers, but had taken no drink for three years." The love of God was beaming in that old man's eyes.

I went on about two hundred yards more. A fine big fellow met me and addressed me by my name. He too, strange to say, said he signed the pledge at my first meeting in Derry three years before. I asked him if he had been a drinker. He said, "Drinker! I think I was a drinker! I was one of the biggest drunkards that ever walked the streets of Derry, and I have never tasted drink since I signed your pledge three years ago." Then, with great tears in his eyes, and his voice almost choked with emotion, he added, "And, your reverence, I could not even begin to tell you all that my pledge means for my wife and my children."

Need I say that I felt inspired to go into the pulpit to preach that day as perhaps I never felt before. I question if there was a minister in Ireland who had such encouragement as I met with in a seemingly accidental way that day on the footpath on my way to church.

One day I met a gentleman in Belfast who told me that over a hundred of the drunkards in his small town were on their feet through this movement. And just a short while before I came to America I addressed a meeting in a town in county Antrim. When I sat down the secretary of the branch got up to make some announcements. He was a young professional man in good standing, but had been going down in drink. He had been saved by this movement and was not ashamed to acknowledge this fact in the most public way. He said, "There are at least one hundred of us, the greatest drunkards of this town, who have been saved by Catch-my-Pal, and we can point to this man on the platform to-night as, in the hand of God, our earthly saviour." I never was so proud in my life as I was then, and at the same time I never felt so humbled, when I thought that God, in His goodness, permitted such a statement to be made about me. But there was something more in store for me. When that secretary had made all the announcements he came over to me at the side of the platform and said, "Don't go away immediately after the close of the meeting, as I have something down there near the door that will cheer you." When the audience had dispersed he brought me down towards the door. There were three or four rows of men sitting there. They all rose up to receive me when I came to them. I asked them to sit down, as we were all pals together. I talked to each man, and then I talked to the "bunch." When they had gone away my friend, the secretary, said, "Do you know, Mr. Patterson, who those men are that you were talking to?" I said I had no idea who they were. "Well," said he, *"nearly every one of those men is a reformed gaol-bird,* set upon his feet by the Catch-my-Pal movement."

It is not given to every man to receive such encouragements as these, and although the way is long and one's thirst for the joys of home is sometimes almost unbearable, God provides these brooks by the way, and one goes on his way rejoicing that the joy of other homes than his own is being increased by his wandering ministry.

CHAPTER XXXVIII

WILL CATCH-MY-PAL LAST?

WILL Catch-my-Pal last? This is a question which greatly troubled many people at the beginning of the movement, especially those who took no active interest in it to make it a permanent success.

At one of our earliest meetings in the schoolroom in Armagh, I said to the men: "Men, the saloon-keepers of the city are saying that this thing will be dead at Christmas; what have you got to say to this?" One man said, "No!" I answered that that was no answer to come from such a body of men to such a vile insinuation from the publicans, and that I wanted them to let no uncertain sound go out from that meeting as to what they thought about the matter. "Come, now, men," I said: "Is this thing going to be dead at Christmas?" The whole meeting shouted a thundering "No!" And the saloon men heard of it, and began to think that they were perhaps a little premature in their judgment of the movement. The men "had a mind to work." They hammered total abstinence into the ribs of the gallant little ship *Catch-my-Pal*, which weathered the Christmas holidays in what was considered a wonderful way for such a speedily built craft.

The critics then said the craft would founder in the General Election of January, 1910, but it rode on the crest of that wave. The prophets began again as Easter and St. Patrick's Day approached, but again they proved to be false prophets. They tried their divinations again when the 12th of July drew near, but somehow the diviners were once more disappointed. There was another election in December, 1910, and it was found that the movement was still increasing the number of happy firesides at Christmas. The critics began to find it was their criticisms that were foundering, and to-day there are living testimonies all over the United Kingdom that indeed a notable miracle has been wrought and the critics can say nothing against it.

I was not so foolish, I hope, as to have thought at any time that the first enthusiasm would last. All such movements are well described in words which I may here adapt for my purpose: "They shall mount up with wings as eagles, they shall run and not be weary, they shall walk and not faint." In many places the movement is still mounting up. In some places it is running. In other places it is walking. In some places the meetings have ceased to be held, but even there the result of the meetings that were held still abides in redeemed lives. For instance, a report comes to me to this effect: "We ran the Catch-my-Pal for some time as a department of our Brotherhood, and although we no longer hold distinct temperance meetings on Catch-my-Pal lines I am thankful to say that your movement was the means of lifting up two great drunkards who, I believe, are saved for all time."

Our Lord summed up His Galilean ministry in the parable of The Sower. *In every revival in the history of the world there have been four kinds of ground—* the wayside, the stony, the thorny, and the good ground. In this revival, while there have been wayside, stony and thorny grounds, there have been wide stretches and far distances of good ground, where as many as thirty, sixty, and, in many cases, eighty per cent. of those who took the pledge have kept it.

Many friends urged me to publish the story of the movement within the first year of its existence, but I thought it was better to delay such a publication till some considerable time had elapsed. If I had published my story early in the history of the work the criticism might very justly have been made: "Oh, this is a nine days' wonder. It won't last. These men and women who have signed the pledge will not continue to keep it." But now, after almost five years of history, I am in a position to relate the stories of lives found in this book, lives that have stood the test and are a standing testimony as to what the Grace of God has done by the hand of Catch-my-Pal. As I have intimated in another chapter, many pledges have been broken; but I have no hesitation in saying that far more pledges have been kept than even the most hopeful of us expected, and that I am continually receiving news of changed lives in Ireland and every land the movement has entered that makes my heart almost cry aloud with joy.

Will the movement last? Unselfish people who are willing to go out of their way to save a fallen brother say it will last. Selfish people who will not go out of their selfish way for any purpose say it will not last. But what the future is going to do with the movement I do not know, and it is not for me to try to divine. It is for me, it is for all of us who say we love God, to love our brothers also, and to do what we can to save the fallen brothers we see about us *to-day*. To-day if we hear God's voice calling us to Good Samaritanship, let us not harden our hearts. We can leave the future of the movement in God's hands, but it is for us to have an understanding of our own times to know what we ought to do. And we ought to lift up the man that is down. *We cannot get away from the fact that this is our duty.* And if we do this duty that lies at our hand to-day we shall make it all the easier for our children to do their duty in their day and generation.

A minister was talking to me about his mother in a most pathetic way. He was a tall man. I listened with becoming gravity, and looked up at him and asked: "Is your mother alive?" He looked down and said in a tone that made my heart almost sink within me: "Ah, no; she's not alive; she's not alive; she's dead. But—*she was alive.*"

I am grateful to say that I cannot thus speak of the Catch-my-Pal movement. If I did there are hundreds of redeemed lives throughout the land that would tell me how I lied.

Beside my brother's manse in county Monaghan, Ireland, is a churchyard. In that churchyard is a vault. On that vault is this inscription (names are changed):

HERE LIE THE REMAINS OF

Mr. AND Mrs. WILLIAM BLANK,

OF THE TOWN AND COUNTY OF MONAGHAN,

BOTH DECEASED.

The remains of the Catch-my-Pal movement are all over the country. But it is noteworthy that these remains are *not deceased.*

Many persons who have been living in drunken sin have forsaken their ways and have returned unto the Lord Who has had mercy on them, and to their God Who has abundantly pardoned. Many persons who used to go out to wallow in the drink gutter and to return to their hearth stones with the music of hell, the drunkard's gurgle, in their throats, have come to know how true are the old words: "Ye shall go out with joy, and be led forth with peace: the mountains and hills shall break forth before you into singing, and all the trees of the field shall clap their hands. Instead of the thorn shall come up the fir tree, and instead of the brier shall come up the myrtle tree: and it shall be to the Lord for a name, for AN EVER-LASTING SIGN THAT SHALL NOT BE CUT OFF."

"I know that safe with Him remains,
 Protected by His power,
What I've committed to His trust
 Till the decisive hour.

"Then will He own His servant's name
 Before His Father's face,
And in the New Jerusalem
 Appoint my soul a place."

APPENDIX

SUMMARY OF METHODS AND OF RESULTS FOR READY REFERENCE

I. METHODS

LET me state some of the leading ideas at the back and heart of the movement:

(1) We do not assume that any man wants to go to hell. We assume that the worst man wants to go to heaven, and we try to give him a chance. He is *a diamond in the rough*, to be cut and polished for the crown of Jesus. I wish this movement to be known as a Good Samaritan of the twentieth century that will pass no man or woman by.

(2) We lay great stress on publicity of pledge-signing. A man will probably fall if he is alone. *The sense of Brotherhood saves.* He will feel on sure ground if he knows he is surrounded by a host of others who are all striving after the same end as himself.

(3) We believe the greatest drinkers are fitted to be the best workers, as they know their pals' temptations and how to approach them with a view to winning them for sobriety. *We ask the men who have been making the problem to go out and solve it.* And certainly we have found our best workers among those who were formerly the worst drinkers. We put the responsibility on the men and women, instead of on the officers.

(4) We believe that there should be counter-attrac-

tions to the saloon in almost every street in our towns, and we have opened many in Ireland. Men do not love the drink so much as they love the fellowship they get in drinking with their friends. If the Christian community would provide up-to-date Temperance saloons, more comfortable in every way than the licensed saloons, these would be patronised in a way that would surprise the most hopeful of us. Men and women say they go to the saloons because they have no other places to go to. If other places were provided in such a way as to attract, instead of to repel, as is often the case, people would be ashamed to be seen going into drink-shops. If they passed a temperance saloon to go into a saloon, it would then be known it was for alcohol they did so, and the sense of shame would assert itself. Public opinion would then have a method of making itself felt. And, after all, it *is public opinion that does the work.*

(5) We have great sympathy with the tempted. They are children in will power. If a child falls down the stairs, why does it fall? Because it was up. Many who sign will fall. They were up. If they were up once, they can be raised up again. And, in this movement, if a man falls, there are plenty of his pals to lift him up again. His rescue is not left to those who are known outstandingly as Christian workers. The officer directs operations, but *the man in the ranks is the most immediate and the best saviour of his fellow.* As often as a man falls we try to lift him up again.

(6) We believe in weekly meetings for recruiting purposes. Enthusiasm is likely to die if it is not often fed. *There are too many men being lost, so we should not lose time.* Meetings, while run on religious lines, should all be as bright and happy as possible, and not necessarily devoted to temperance all the time. The interest of men and women in all sorts of subjects should be fostered. At every meeting, after the new recruits are enrolled, all present repeat the pledge after

the President. The pledge is: "For God and Home and country, I promise, by God's help, to abstain from all intoxicating drinks as beverages, and to do all that in me lies to promote the cause of Total Abstinence by getting others to join the Union." After the repetition of the Pledge with uplifted hand, all members shut their hands as the sign of Christian determination and say word by word in unison:

"WE—WILL—SEE—THIS—THING—
THROUGH."

II.—RESULTS

The movement has, in many respects, exceeded the expectations of even its most sanguine supporters. From all quarters the remarkable testimony comes to me that generally the worst drinkers are proving themselves the best pledge-keepers. Those in "the Trade" expected the crusade to collapse at Christmas, 1909. But it did not. Then it was prophesied it would collapse at the General Election in January, 1910. But it did not. Other holidays and extraordinary occasions were being looked to in 1910 for an indication that Catch-my-Pal would fall; but it firmly held its ground through them all, and now, at the end of five years, it continues as a means of blessing to homes all over the United Kingdom and in many other parts of the world.

(1) The movement has given temperance workers a new hope. It has been proved that work among the drunkards and drinkers is not so hopeless as was once thought. It is a characteristic of this movement that it gathers up most of the worst cases in every town it enters. *The children of the drinkers who are being reclaimed now have an example at the fireside which will be far more potent in its preventive and saving*

227

influence than all the temperance addresses that were ever delivered. Once we win the drinkers we shall have their children as well.

(2) The movement has united the churches in Ireland. It bids fair to be the means of opening up a way from the heart of one church to that of another. The spirit of brotherhood which has manifested itself among the members of the Union, chiefly through the wearing of the little badge, is proving a potent factor in the union of the churches.

(3) The movement is becoming a feeder of the churches. People who never came to church, because of their indulgence in drink, are reported as becoming staunch church members. The gulf between the churches and the labouring men is being bridged. *The men are all looking to the ministers as their natural leaders in the movement, and where ministers have not given the lead men are filled with a wonderful curiosity as to the reason why.*

(4) The movement is manifesting many spiritual signs. From all over the land I receive word of great drinkers becoming devoted servants of Our Lord. We are not content to stop with mere total abstinence. We aim at securing the whole man for God and purity of life. Our bodies are the temples of the Holy Ghost. The movement is religious at heart, as all reform movements must be if they are to be truly successful.

(5) The movement has worked and is working wonders on the material side of life. This is seen in the better clothing of those who used to spend nearly their all in drink, and also in much cleaner houses, better spread tables, clear rent-books, and "squared" grocers' bills.

In many places the Catch-my-Pal has proved to be a drink-quake. As a speaker said in the General Assembly of the Irish Presbyterian Church: "One thing is sure, that however certain persons may minimise or under-estimate the work, our enemy does not belittle it. The opposition of 'the Trade' is the clear proof of its consternation. Usually it is quietly contemptuous of temperance meetings and temperance work, but this crusade it hates like poison, and uses every means to discredit and weaken it. No wonder, when the results are such as they are!"

The responsibility of saving the community from drink is left on the shoulders of the members. Ministers and other Christian workers can never overtake the programme unless every man and every woman does his and her duty. Wellington could not have won Waterloo or Nelson Trafalgar, if the rank and file on the field and fleet had not done their duty. The people have the problem in the hollow of their hand. Would to God they would respond to the call, and rise and smite and slay and "destroy the works of the devil." Jesus Christ founded His Church for this purpose. Let us carry out His purpose, and He will bless His people with peace, joy, purity, prosperity, and love, such as they have never experienced before.

We hope there will be no sounding of retreat by the Catch-my-Pal bugle till every city, and town, and village, and hamlet in America is won for Total Abstinence. God Almighty wants to save this great country from its greatest foe, and who will say He is not going to work towards this end by the instrument called "Catch-my-Pal," which means *sympathy, brotherhood, and the heart of fire?*

WAKE UP, UNITED STATES!!
AND
SEE THIS THING THROUGH!!

Lightning Source UK Ltd.
Milton Keynes UK
UKHW021847190521
384027UK00003B/180